# www.EffortlessMath.com

... So Much More Online!

✓ FREE Math lessons

✓ More Math learning books!

✓ Mathematics Worksheets

✓ Online Math Tutors

**Need a PDF version of this book?**

Please visit www.EffortlessMath.com

# CLEP College Algebra Prep 2020

## *A Comprehensive Review and Step-By-Step Guide to Preparing for the CLEP College Algebra Test*

By

Reza Nazari & Ava Ross

All inquiries should be addressed to:

info@effortlessMath.com

www.EffortlessMath.com

**ISBN-13:** 978-1-64612-155-7

**ISBN-10:** 1-64612-155-4

**Published by: Effortless Math Education**

**www.EffortlessMath.com**

## Description

***CLEP College Algebra Prep 2020,*** which reflects the 2020 CLEP College Algebra test guidelines, provides students with the confidence and math skills they need to ace the CLEP College Algebra test. This comprehensive Prep book with hundreds of examples, over 2,500 sample questions, and two full length CLEP College Algebra tests is all you will ever need to fully prepare for the CLEP College Algebra. It will help you hone your math skills, overcome your exam anxiety, and boost your confidence -- and do your best to succeed on the CLEP College Algebra Test.

Whether you are intimidated by math, or even if you were the first to raise your hand in the Algebra classes, this book can help you incorporate the most effective method and the right strategies to prepare for the CLEP College Algebra test successfully. **CLEP College Algebra *Prep 2020*** is a breakthrough in Algebra learning — offering a winning formula and the most powerful methods for learning basic Algebra topics confidently.

The surest way to succeed on CLEP College Algebra Test is with intensive practice in every math topic tested--and that's what you will get in **CLEP College Algebra *Prep 2020*.** Each chapter of this focused format has a comprehensive review created by Test Prep experts that goes into detail to cover all of the content likely to appear on the CLEP College Algebra test. Not only does this all-inclusive workbook offer everything you will ever need to conquer CLEP College Algebra test, it also contains two full-length and realistic CLEP College Algebra tests that reflect the format and question types on the CLEP College Algebra to help you check your exam-readiness and identify where you need more practice.

Inside the pages of this comprehensive prep book, students can learn Algebra topics in a structured manner with a complete study program to help them understand essential Algebra skills. It also has many exciting features, including:

- Content 100% aligned with the 2020 CLEP College Algebra test
- Written by CLEP College Algebra tutors and test experts
- Complete coverage of all CLEP College Algebra concepts and topics which you will be tested
- Step-by-step guide for all CLEP College Algebra topics
- Over 2,500 additional CLEP College Algebra practice questions in both multiple-choice and grid-in formats with answers grouped by topic, so you can focus on your weak areas
- Abundant Math skill building exercises to help test-takers approach different question types that might be unfamiliar to them
- 2 full-length practice tests (featuring new question types) with detailed answers

**CLEP College Algebra Prep 2020 is the only book you'll ever need to master Basic Math topics!** It can be used as a self–study course – you do not need to work with a Algebra tutor. (It can also be used with a Math tutor)

**Ideal for self-study as well as for classroom usage.**

## About the Author

**Reza Nazari** is the author of more than 100 Math learning books including:
– **Math and Critical Thinking Challenges:** For the Middle and High School Student
– **GED Math in 30 Days**
– **ASVAB Math Workbook 2018 - 2019**
– **Effortless Math Education Workbooks**
– **and many more Mathematics books ...**

Reza is also an experienced Math instructor and a test–prep expert who has been tutoring students since 2008. Reza is the founder of Effortless Math Education, a tutoring company that has helped many students raise their standardized test scores—and attend the colleges of their dreams. Reza provides an individualized custom learning plan and the personalized attention that makes a difference in how students view math.

You can contact Reza via email at:
reza@EffortlessMath.com

Find Reza's professional profile at:
goo.gl/zoC9rJ

# Contents

# Chapter 1: Fundamentals and Building Blocks

**Topics that you'll learn in this chapter:**

- ✓ The Order of Operation
- ✓ Scientific Notation
- ✓ Exponents Operations
- ✓ Sets
- ✓ Evaluating Expressions
- ✓ Simplifying Algebraic Expressions

*"A Man is like a fraction whose numerator is what he is and whose denominator is what he thinks of himself. The larger the denominator, the smaller the fraction." – Tolstoy*

# Order of Operations

**Step-by-step guide:**

When there is more than one math operation, use PEMDAS:

- ✓ Parentheses

- ✓ Exponents

- ✓ Multiplication and Division (from left to right)

- ✓ Addition and Subtraction (from left to right)

**Examples:**

1) Solve. $(2 + 4) \div (2^2 \div 4) =$

First simplify inside parentheses: $(6) \div (4 \div 4) = (6) \div (1) =$
Then: $(6) \div (1) = 6$

2) Solve. $(9 \times 6) - (10 - 6) =$

First simplify inside parentheses: $(9 \times 6) - (10 - 6) = (54) - (4) =$

Then: $(54) - (4) = 50$

✎ *Evaluate each expression.*

1) $12 + (3 \times 2) =$

2) $8 - (4 \times 5) =$

3) $(8 \times 2) + 14 =$

4) $(10 - 6) - (4 \times 3) =$

5) $15 + (12 \div 2) =$

6) $(24 \times 3) \div 4 =$

7) $(28 \div 2) \times (-4) =$

8) $(2 \times 6) + (14 - 8) =$

9) $45 + (4 \times 2) + 12 =$

10) $(10 \times 5) \div (4 + 1) =$

11) $(-6) + (8 \times 6) + 10 =$

12) $(12 \times 4) - (56 \div 4) =$

# Scientific Notation

**Step-by-step guide:**

- ✓ It is used to write very big or very small numbers in decimal form.
- ✓ In scientific notation all numbers are written in the form of:

$$m \times 10^n$$

| Decimal notation | Scientific notation |
|---|---|
| 5 | $5 \times 10^0$ |
| – 25,000 | $– 2.5 \times 10^4$ |
| 0.5 | $5 \times 10^{-1}$ |
| 2,122.456 | $2,122456 \times 10^{-3}$ |

***Example:***

1) ***Write*** $0.00015$ ***in scientific notation.***

First, move the decimal point to the right so that you have a number that is between 1 and 10. Then: $N = 1.5$

Second, determine how many places the decimal moved in step 1 by the power of 10.

Then: $10^{-4} \rightarrow$ When the decimal moved to the right, the exponent is negative.

Then: $0.00015 = 1.5 \times 10^{-4}$

2) ***Write*** $9.5 \times 10^{-5}$ ***in standard notation.***

$10^{-5} \rightarrow$ When the decimal moved to the right, the exponent is negative.

Then: $9.5 \times 10^{-5} = 0.000095$

✍ ***Write each number in scientific notation.***

1) $15,000,000 =$

2) $67,000 =$

3) $0.000819 =$

4) $0.00092 =$

✍ ***Write each number in standard notation.***

5) $4.5 \times 10^3 =$

6) $8 \times 10^{-4} =$

7) $6 \times 10^{-1} =$

8) $9 \times 10^{-2} =$

# Exponents Operations

**Step-by-step guide:**

- ✓ Exponents are shorthand for repeated multiplication of the same number by itself. For example, instead of $2 \times 2$, we can write $2^2$. For $3 \times 3 \times 3 \times 3$, we can write $3^4$
- ✓ In algebra, a variable is a letter used to stand for a number. The most common letters are: $x, y, z, a, b, c, m, and\ n$.
- ✓ Exponent's rules: $x^a \times x^b = x^{a+b}$ , $\frac{x^a}{x^b} = x^{a-b}$

$$(x^a)^b = x^{a \times b}, \qquad (xy)^a = x^a \times y^a , (\frac{a}{b})^c = \frac{a^c}{b^c}$$

*Examples:*

1) **Multiply.** $4x^3 \times 2x^2 =$

Use Exponent's rules: $x^a \times x^b = x^{a+b} \rightarrow x^3 \times x^2 = x^{3+2} = x^5$

Then: $4x^3 \times 2x^2 = 8x^5$

2) **Multiply.** $(x^3y^5\ )^2 =$

Use Exponent's rules: $(x^a)^b = x^{a \times b}$. Then: $(x^3y^5\ )^2 = x^{3 \times 2}y^{5 \times 2} = x^6y^{10}$

✎ *Simplify and write the answer in exponential form.*

1) $2x^2 \times 4x =$

2) $5x^4 \times x^2 =$

3) $8x^4 \times 3x^5 =$

4) $3x^2 \times 6xy =$

5) $2x^5y \times 4x^2y^3 =$

6) $9x^2y^5 \times 5x^2y^8 =$

7) $5x^2y \times 5x^2y^7 =$

8) $7x^6 \times 3x^9y^4 =$

9) $8x^8y^5 \times 7x^5y^3 =$

10) $9x^6x^2 \times 4xy^5 =$

11) $12xy^7 \times 2x^9y^8 =$

12) $9x^9y^{12} \times 9x^{14}y^{11} =$

# Sets

**Step-by-step guide:**

- ✓ A set is a collection of objects and each object is an "element" in the set.
- ✓ Set Notation: A set is denoted by a capital letter, such as A, B, or C etc. The list of a set elements enclosed in braces: {...}
- ✓ Set Operations: The union (with the sing ∪) of two sets is the set of elements that belong to one or both of the two sets. The intersection of two sets (with the sing ∩) is the set of elements that are common to both sets.

**Example:**

1) *If* $A = \{2, 5, 11, 15\}$, $B = \{1, 2, 3, 4, 5, 6\}$, *and* $C = \{5, 7, 9, 11, 13\}$, *then which of the following set is* $(A \cup B) \cap C$?

A. $\{1, 2, 3, 4, 5, 6, 11, 15\}$      C. $\{5, 11, 13, 15\}$

B. $\{1, 2, 3, 4, 5, 6, 7, 11, 13, 15\}$      D. $\{5, 11\}$

**Answer:** Choice D is correct. The union of $A$ and $B$ is: $A \cup B = \{1, 2, 3, 4, 5, 6, 11, 15\}$
The intersection of $(A \cup B)$ and $C$ is: $(A \cup B) \cap C = \{5, 11\}$, because only 5 and 11 are common to both sets of $(A \cup B)$ and $C$.

✎ *Given* $A = \{1, 2, 3, 8, 12\}$, $B = \{2, 4, 5, 7\}$, *and* $C = \{5, 7, 9, 11\}$, **find:**

1) $A \cup B$ _____      6) $B \cap C$ _____

2) $A \cup C$ _____      7) $(A \cup B) \cup C$ _____

3) $B \cup C$ _____      8) $(A \cup B) \cap C$ _____

4) $A \cap B$ _____      9) $(A \cap B) \cap C$ _____

5) $A \cap C$ _____      10) $(B \cup C) \cap A$ _____

## Evaluating Expressions

**Step-by-step guide:**

✓ To evaluate an algebraic expression, substitute a number for each variable and perform the arithmetic operations.

**Examples:**

2) **Solve this expression.** $4(2a - b), a = 2, b = -1$

First substitute 2 for $a$, and $-1$ for $b$ , then:

$4(2a - b), 8a - 4b = 8(2) - 4(-1) = 16 + 4 = 20$

3) **Solve this expression.** $2x + 6y, x = 1, y = 2$

First substitute 1 for $x$, and 2 for $y$ , then:

$2x + 6y = 2(1) + 6(2) = 2 + 12 = 14$

✎ *Evaluate each expression using the values given.*

1) $x + 2y,$
$x = 1, y = 2$

2) $2x - 3y,$
$x = 1, y = -2$

3) $-a + 5b,$
$a = -2, b = 3$

4) $-3a + 5b,$
$a = 5, b = 2$

5) $5x + 8 - 3y,$
$x = 5, y = 4$

6) $3x + 5y,$
$x = 2, y = 3$

7) $7x + 6y,$
$x = 2, y = 4$

8) $3a - (12 - b),$
$a = 3, b = 5$

9) $4z + 20 + 7k,$
$z = -4, k = 5$

10) $xy + 15 + 4x,$
$x = 6, y = 3$

11) $8x + 3 - 5y + 4,$
$x = 6, y = 3$

12) $5 + 2(-3x - 4y),$
$x = 6, y = 5$

# Simplifying Algebraic Expressions

**Step-by-step guide:**

- ✓ In algebra, a variable is a letter used to stand for a number. The most common letters are: $x, y, z, a, b, c, m, and\ n$.
- ✓ algebraic expression is an expression contains integers, variables, and the math operations such as addition, subtraction, multiplication, division, etc.
- ✓ In an expression, we can combine "like" terms. (values with same variable and same power)

**Examples:**

1) Simplify this expression. $(2x + 3x + 4) =$?
   Combine like terms. Then: $(2x + 3x + 4) = 5x + 4$ (remember you cannot combine variables and numbers.
2) Simplify this expression. $12 - 3x^2 + 5x + 4x^2 =$?
   Combine "like" terms: $-3x^2 + 4x^2 = x^2$

   Then: $= 12 + x^2 + 5x$. Write in standard form (biggest powers first): $x^2 + 5x + 12$

✎ *Simplify each expression.*

1) $x - 4 + 6 - 2x =$

2) $3 - 4x + 14 - 3x =$

3) $33x - 5 + 13 + 4x =$

4) $-3 - x^2 - 7x^2 =$

5) $4 + 11x^2 + 3 =$

6) $7x^2 + 5x + 6x^2 =$

7) $42x + 15 + 3x^2 =$

8) $6x(x - 2) - 5 =$

9) $7x - 6 + 9x + 3x^2 =$

10) $(-5)(7x - 2) + 12x =$

11) $15x - 6(6 - 7x) =$

12) $25x + 6(7x + 2) + 14 =$

# Answers – Chapter 1

## Order of Operations

1) 18
2) −12
3) 30
4) −8

5) 21
6) 18
7) −56
8) 18

9) 65
10) 10
11) 52
12) 34

## Scientific Notation

1) $1.5 \times 10^7$
2) $6.7 \times 10^4$
3) $8.19 \times 10^{-4}$
4) $9.2 \times 10^{-4}$

5) 4,500
6) 0.0008
7) 0.6
8) 0.09

## Exponents Operations

1) $8x^3$
2) $5x^6$
3) $24x^9$
4) $18x^3y$

5) $8x^7y^4$
6) $45x^4y^{13}$
7) $25x^4y^8$
8) $21x^{15}y^4$

9) $56x^{13}y^8$
10) $36x^9y^5$
11) $24x^{10}y^{15}$
12) $81x^{23}y^{23}$

## Sets

1) $\{1, 2, 3, 4, 5, 7, 8, 12\}$
2) $\{1, 2, 3, 5, 7, 8, 9, 11, 12\}$
3) $\{2, 4, 5, 7, 9, 11\}$
4) $\{2\}$
5) $\{\ \ \}$ *(empty set)*

6) $\{5, 7\}$
7) $\{1, 2, 3, 4, 5, 7, 8, 9, 11, 12\}$
8) $\{5, 7\}$
9) $\{\ \ \}$ *(empty set)*
10) $\{2\}$

## Evaluating Expressions

1) 5
2) 8
3) 17
4) −5

5) 21
6) 21
7) 38
8) 2

9) 39
10) 57
11) 40
12) −71

## Simplifying Algebraic Expressions

1) $-x + 2$
2) $-7x + 17$
3) $37x + 8$
4) $-8x^2 - 3$
5) $11x^2 + 7$
6) $13x^2 + 5x$

7) $3x^2 + 42x + 15$
8) $6x^2 - 12x - 5$
9) $3x^2 + 16x - 6$
10) $-23x + 10$
11) $57x - 36$
12) $67x + 26$

# Chapter 2:
# Equations and Inequalities

**Math Topics that you'll learn in this chapter:**

- ✓ One–Step Equations

- ✓ Multi–Step Equations

- ✓ Graphing Single–Variable Inequalities

- ✓ One–Step Inequalities

- ✓ Multi–Step Inequalities

*"Life is a math equation. In order to gain the most, you have to know how to convert negatives into positives."*

*- Anonymous*

# One–Step Equations

**Step-by-step guide:**

✓ The values of two expressions on both sides of an equation are equal. $ax + b = c$
✓ You only need to perform one Math operation in order to solve the one-step equations.
✓ To solve one-step equation, find the inverse (opposite) operation is being performed.
✓ The inverse operations are:
  - Addition and subtraction
  - Multiplication and division

**Examples:**

1) **Solve this equation.**  $2x = 16, x = ?$
   Here, the operation is multiplication (variable $x$ is multiplied by 3) and its inverse operation is division. To solve this equation, divide both sides of **equation by** 2:
   $$2x = 16 \rightarrow 2x \div 2 = 16 \div 2 \rightarrow x = 8$$

2) **Solve this equation.**  $x + 12 = 0 , x = ?$
   Here, the operation is addition and its inverse operation is subtraction. To solve this equation, subtract 12 from both sides of the **equation:** $x + 12 - 12 = 0 - 12$
   Then simplify: $x + 12 - 12 = 0 - 12 \rightarrow x = -12$

✎ *Solve each equation.*

1) $14 = -2 + x, x =$ ____

2) $x + 7 = 14, x =$ ____

3) $x - 3 = 15, x =$ ____

4) $6 = 14 + x, x =$ ____

5) $x - 4 = 5, x =$ ____

6) $3 - x = -11, x =$ ____

7) $x - 5 = -15, x =$ ____

8) $x - 14 = 14, x =$ ____

9) $x - 15 = -30, x =$ ____

10) $x - 12 = 34, x =$ ____

11) $9 - x = 5, x =$ ____

12) $x - 16 = 16, x =$ ____

# Multi–Step Equations

**Step-by-step guide:**

- ✓ Combine "like" terms on one side.
- ✓ Bring variables to one side by adding or subtracting.
- ✓ Simplify using the inverse of addition or subtraction.
- ✓ Simplify further by using the inverse of multiplication or division.

**Examples:**

1) **Solve this equation.** $-(8 - x) = 6$

First use Distributive Property: $-(8 - x) = -8 + x$

Now solve by subtract 6 to both sides of the equation. $-8 + x = 6 \rightarrow -8 + x - 6 = 6 - 6$

Now simplify: $-14 + x = 0 \rightarrow x = 14$

2) **Solve this equation.** $2x + 5 = 15 - x$

First bring variables to one side by adding $x$ to both sides.

$2x + 5 = 15 - x \rightarrow 3x + 5 = 15$. Now, subtract 15 from both sides:

$3x + 5 - 15 = 15 - 15 \rightarrow 3x - 10 = 0 \rightarrow 3x = 10$

Now, divide both sides by 3: $3x = 10 \rightarrow 3x \div 3 = \frac{10}{3} \rightarrow x = \frac{10}{3}$

✍ **Solve each equation.**

1) $-(3 - x) = 7$

2) $3x - 15 = 12$

3) $3x - 3 = 9$

4) $3x - 15 = 6$

5) $-3(5 + x) = 3$

6) $-5(3 + x) = 5$

7) $24 = -(x - 7)$

8) $6(4 - 2x) = 30$

9) $18 - 4x = -9 - x$

10) $14 - 2x = 14 + x$

11) $30 + 15x = -6 + 3x$

12) $18 = (-4x) - 9 + 3$

# Graphing Single–Variable Inequalities

**Step-by-step guide:**

✓ Inequality is similar to equations and uses symbols for "less than" (<) and "greater than" (>).
✓ To solve inequalities, we need to isolate the variable. (like in equations)
✓ To graph an inequality, find the value of the inequality on the number line.
✓ For less than or greater than draw open circle on the value of the variable.
✓ If there is an equal sign too, then use filled circle.
✓ Draw a line to the right or to the left for greater or less than.

**Examples:**

1) **Draw a graph for** $x > 4$

Since, the variable is greater than 4, then we need to find 4 and draw an open circle above it. Then, draw a line to the right.

2) **Graph this inequality.** $x < 5$

✎ *Draw a graph for each inequality.*

1) $x > 2$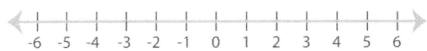

2) $x < -2$

3) $x < 4$

4) $x > -1$

5) $x < 5$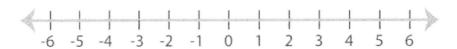

# One–Step Inequalities

**Step-by-step guide:**

- ✓ Similar to equations, first isolate the variable by using inverse operation.
- ✓ For dividing or multiplying both sides by negative numbers, flip the direction of the inequality sign.

**Examples:**

1) **Solve and graph the inequality.** $x + 2 \geq 3$.

Subtract 2 from both sides. $x + 2 \geq 3 \rightarrow x + 2 - 2 \geq 3 - 2$, then: $x \geq 1$

2) **Solve this inequality.** $x - 1 \leq 2$

Add 1 to both sides. $x - 1 \leq 2 \rightarrow x - 1 + 1 \leq 2 + 1$, then: $x \leq 3$

✍ *Solve each inequality and graph it.*

1) $4x \geq 8$

2) $2 + x \leq 6$

3) $x + 4 \leq 9$

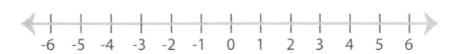

4) $8x \geq 24$

5) $5x \leq 20$

# Multi–Step Inequalities

**Step-by-step guide:**

✓ Isolate the variable.
✓ Simplify using the inverse of addition or subtraction.
✓ Simplify further by using the inverse of multiplication or division.

**Examples:**

1) **Solve this inequality.** $x - 2 \leq 4$

First add 2 to both sides: $x - 2 + 2 \leq 4 + 2 \rightarrow x \leq 6$

2) **Solve this inequality.** $2x + 6 \leq 10$

First add 4 to both sides: $2x + 6 - 6 \leq 10 - 6$

Then simplify: $2x + 6 - 6 \leq 10 - 6 \rightarrow 2x \leq 4$

Now divide both sides by 2: $\frac{2x}{2} \leq \frac{4}{2} \rightarrow x \leq 2$

✎ **Solve each inequality.**

1) $x - 5 \leq 4$

2) $2x - 2 \leq 12$

3) $3 + 2x \leq 11$

4) $x - 6 \geq 12$

5) $3x - 6 \leq 12$

6) $7x - 3 \leq 18$

7) $2x - 3 < 23$

8) $15 - 2x \geq -15$

9) $7 + 3x < 25$

10) $2 + 4x \geq 18$

11) $7 + 3x < 34$

12) $5x - 2 < 8$

# Answers – Chapter 2

## *One–Step Equations*

1) 16
2) 7
3) 18
4) −8
5) 9
6) 14

7) −10
8) 28
9) −15
10) 46
11) 4
12) 32

## *Multi–Step Equations*

1) 10
2) 9
3) 4
4) 7
5) −6
6) −4
7) −17

8) $-\frac{1}{2}$
9) 9
10) 0
11) −3
12) −6

## *Graphing Single–Variable Inequalities*

1)

2)

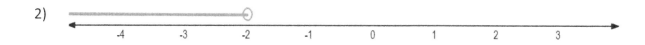

3)

4)

5)

## One–Step Inequalities

1)

2)

3)

4)

5)

## Multi–Step inequalities

1) $x \leq 9$
2) $x \leq 7$
3) $x \leq 4$
4) $x \geq 18$
5) $x \leq 6$
6) $x \leq 3$

7) $x < 13$
8) $x \leq 15$
9) $x < 6$
10) $x \geq 4$
11) $x < 9$
12) $x < 2$

# Chapter 3:
# System of Equations and Quadratic

**Topics that you'll learn in this chapter:**

- ✓ Solving Systems of Equations

- ✓ Systems of Equations Word Problems

- ✓ Solve a Quadratic Equation

- ✓ Graphing Quadratic Functions in Vertex Form

- ✓ Solving Quadratic Equations

- ✓ Solve Quadratic Inequalities

- ✓ Graphing Quadratic Inequalities

*"Do not worry about your difficulties in mathematics. I can assure you mine are still greater." ~ Albert Einstein*

# Systems of Equations

**Step-by-step guide:**

- ✓ A system of equations contains two equations and two variables. For example, consider the system of equations: $x - y = 1, x + y = 5$
- ✓ The easiest way to solve a system of equation is using the elimination method. The elimination method uses the addition property of equality. You can add the same value to each side of an equation.
- ✓ For the first equation above, you can add $x + y$ to the left side and 5 to the right side of the first equation: $x - y + (x + y) = 1 + 5$. Now, if you simplify, you get: $x - y + (x + y) = 1 + 5 \rightarrow 2x = 6 \rightarrow x = 3$. Now, substitute 3 for the $x$ in the first equation: $3 - y = 1$. By solving this equation, $y = 2$

**Example:**

What is the value of $x + y$ in this system of equations? $\begin{cases} 2x + 5y = 11 \\ 4x - 2y = -26 \end{cases}$

Solving Systems of Equations by Elimination

Multiply the first equation by $(-2)$, then add it to the second equation.

$$\begin{matrix} -2(2x + 5y = 11) \\ 4x - 2y = -26 \end{matrix} \Rightarrow \begin{matrix} -4x - 10y = -22 \\ 4x - 2y = -26 \end{matrix} \Rightarrow -12y = -48 \Rightarrow y = 4$$

Plug in the value of $y$ into one of the equations and solve for $x$.

$2x + 5(4) = 11 \Rightarrow 2x + 20 = 11 \Rightarrow 2x = -9 \Rightarrow x = -4.5$

Thus, $x + y = -4.5 + 4 = -0.5$

## ✎ Solve each system of equations.

1) $-4x - 6y = 7$      $x = $ ____
   $x - 2y = 7$      $y = $ ____

2) $-5x + y = -3$      $x = $ ____
   $3x - 7y = 21$      $y = $ ____

3) $3y = -6x + 12$      $x = $ ____
   $8x - 9y = -10$      $y = $ ____

4) $x + 15y = 50$      $x = $ ____
   $x + 10y = 40$      $y = $ ____

5) $3x - 2y = 15$      $x = $ ____
   $3x - 5y = 15$      $y = $ ____

6) $3x - 6y = -12$      $x = $ ____
   $-x - 3y = -6$      $y = $ ____

# Systems of Equations Word Problems

**Step-by-step guide:**

✓ Define your variables, write two equations, and use elimination method for solving systems of equations.

**Example:**

Tickets to a movie cost $8 for adults and $5 for students. A group of friends purchased **20** tickets for $115.00. How many adults ticket did they buy? _____

Let $x$ be the number of adult tickets and $y$ be the number of student tickets. There are 20 tickets. Then: $x + y = 20$. The cost of adults' tickets is $8 and for students it is $5, and the total cost is $115. So, $8x + 5y = 115$. Now, we have a system of equations: $\begin{cases} x + y = 20 \\ 8x + 5y = 115 \end{cases}$

Multiply the first equation by $-5$ and add to the second equation: $-5(x + y = 20) = -5x - 5y = -100$

$8x + 5y + (-5x - 5y) = 115 - 100 \rightarrow 3x = 15 \rightarrow x = 5 \rightarrow 5 + y = 20 \rightarrow y = 15$. There are 5 adult tickets and 15 student tickets.

✎ *Solve each word problem.*

1) A theater is selling tickets for a performance. Mr. Smith purchased 8 senior tickets and 5 child tickets for $136 for his friends and family. Mr. Jackson purchased 4 senior tickets and 6 child tickets for $96. What is the price of a senior ticket? $_____

2) The difference of two numbers is 6. Their sum is 14. What is the bigger number? $_____

3) The sum of the digits of a certain two-digit number is 7. Reversing its digits increase the number by 9. What is the number? _____

4) The difference of two numbers is 18. Their sum is 66. What are the numbers? _____

# Solving a Quadratic Equation

**Step-by-step guide:**

- ✓ Write the equation in the form of: $ax^2 + bx + c = 0$
- ✓ Factorize the quadratic and solve for the variable.
- ✓ Use quadratic formula if you couldn't factorize the quadratic.
- ✓ Quadratic formula: $x = \frac{-b \pm \sqrt{b^2 - 4ac}}{2a}$

## Examples:

Find the solutions of each quadratic.

1)  $x^2 + 7x + 10 = 0$

   **Use quadratic formula:** $= \frac{-b \pm \sqrt{b^2 - 4ac}}{2a}$, $a = 1, b = 7$ and $c = 10$

   $x = \frac{-7 \pm \sqrt{7^2 - 4.1.10}}{2.1}$, $x_1 = \frac{-7 + \sqrt{7^2 - 4.1.10}}{2.1} = -2$, $x_2 = \frac{-7 - \sqrt{7^2 - 4.1.10}}{2.1} = -5$

2)  $x^2 + 4x + 3 = 0$

   **Use quadratic formula:** $= \frac{-b \pm \sqrt{b^2 - 4ac}}{2a}$, $a = 1, b = 4$ and $c = 3$

   then: $x = \frac{-4 \pm \sqrt{4^2 - 4.1(3)}}{2(1)}$, $x_1 = \frac{-4 + \sqrt{4^2 - 4.1(3)}}{2(1)} = -1$, $x_2 = \frac{-4 - \sqrt{4^2 - 4.1(3)}}{2(1)} = -3$

✏ *Solve each equation.*

1) $x^2 - 5x - 14 = 0$

2) $x^2 + 8x + 15 = 0$

3) $x^2 - 5x - 36 = 0$

4) $x^2 - 12x - 35 = 0$

5) $x^2 + 12x + 32 = 0$

6) $5x^2 + 27x + 28 = 0$

7) $8x^2 + 26x + 15 = 0$

8) $3x^2 + 10x + 8 = 0$

9) $12x^2 + 30x + 12 = 0$

10) $9x^2 + 57x + 18 = 0$

# Graphing Quadratic Functions

**Step-by-step guide:**

- ✓ Quadratic functions in vertex form: $y = a(x - h)^2 + k$ where $(h, k)$ is the vertex of the function. The axis of symmetry is $x = h$
- ✓ Quadratic functions in standard form: $y = ax^2 + bx + c$ where $x = -\frac{b}{2a}$ is the value of $x$ in the vertex of the function.
- ✓ To graph a quadratic function, first find the vertex, then substitute some values for $x$ and solve for $y$.

## Example:

*Sketch the graph of* $y = (x + 1)^2 - 2$.

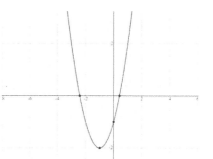

*The vertex of* $y = (x + 1)^2 - 2$ *is* $(-1, -2)$. Substitute zero for $x$ and solve for $y$. $y = (0 + 1)^2 - 2 = -1$. The $y$ Intercept is $(0, -1)$.

Now, you can simply graph the quadratic function.

✍️ *Sketch the graph of each function. Identify the vertex and axis of symmetry.*

1) $y = 3(x - 5)^2 - 2$

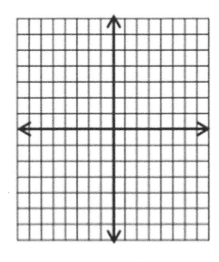

2) $y = x^2 - 3x + 15$

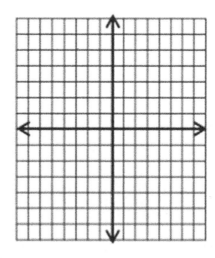

# Solving Quadratic Inequalities

**Step-by-step guide:**

✓ A quadratic inequality is one that can be written in one of the following standard forms:

$$ax^2 + bx + c > 0, \ ax^2 + bx + c < 0, \ ax^2 + bx + c \geq 0, \ ax^2 + bx + c \leq 0$$

✓ Solving a quadratic inequality is like solving equations. We need to find the solutions.

## Examples:

1) ***Solve quadratic inequality.*** $x^2 - 6x + 8 > 0$

   Factor: $x^2 - 6x + 8 > 0 \rightarrow (x - 2)(x - 4) > 0$

   Then the solution could be $x < 2$ or $x > 4$.

2) ***Solve quadratic inequality.*** $x^2 - 7x + 10 \geq 0$

   Factor: $x^2 - 7x + 10 \geq 0 \rightarrow (x - 2)(x - 5) \geq 0$. 2 and 5 are the solutions. Now, the solution could be $x < 2$ or $x = 2$ and $x = 5$ or $x > 5$.

✍ *Solve each quadratic inequality.*

1) $x^2 + 7x + 10 < 0$

7) $x^2 - 16x + 64 \geq 0$

2) $x^2 + 9x + 20 > 0$

8) $x^2 - 36 \leq 0$

3) $x^2 - 8x + 16 > 0$

9) $x^2 - 13x + 36 \geq 0$

4) $x^2 - 8x + 12 \leq 0$

10) $x^2 + 15x + 36 \leq 0$

5) $x^2 - 11x + 30 \leq 0$

11) $4x^2 - 6x - 9 > x^2$

6) $x^2 - 12x + 27 \geq 0$

12) $5x^2 - 15x + 10 < 0$

# Graphing Quadratic inequalities

**Step-by-step guide:**

- ✓ A quadratic inequality is in the form $y > ax^2 + bx + c$ (or substitute $<, \leq,$ or $\geq$ for $>$).
- ✓ To graph a quadratic inequality, start by graphing the quadratic parabola. Then fill in the region either inside or outside of it, depending on the inequality.
- ✓ Choose a testing point and check the solution section.

**Example:** *Sketch the graph of $y > 3x^2$.*

First, graph $y = 3x^2$

Since, the inequality sing is $>$, we need to use dash lines.

Now, choose a testing point inside the parabola. Let's choose (0,2). $\qquad y > 3x^2 \rightarrow 2 > 3(0)^2 \rightarrow 3 > 0$

This is true. So, inside the parabola is the solution section.

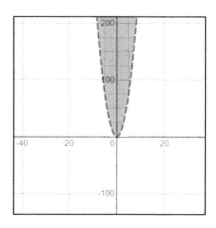

✎ *Sketch the graph of each function.*

1) $y < -2x^2$

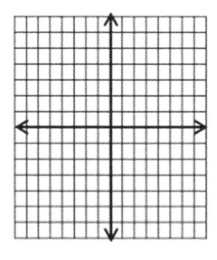

2) $y \geq 4x^2$

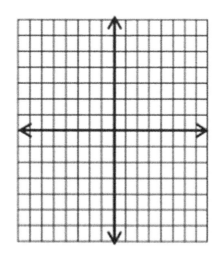

# Answers – Chapter 3

## Systems of Equations

1) $x = 2, y = -\frac{5}{2}$
2) $x = 0, y = -3$
3) $x = 1, y = 2$
4) $x = 20, y = 2$
5) $x = 5, y = 0$
6) $x = 0, y = 2$

## Systems of Equations Word Problems

1) $12
2) 10
3) 34
4) 42, 24

## Solving a Quadratic Equation

1) $x = -2, x = 7$
2) $x = -3, x = -5$
3) $x = 9, x = -4$
4) $x = 7, x = 5$
5) $x = -4, x = -8$
6) $x = -\frac{7}{5}, x = -4$
7) $x = -\frac{5}{2}, x = -\frac{3}{4}$
8) $x = -\frac{4}{3}, x = -2$
9) $x = -\frac{1}{2}, x = -2$
10) $x = -\frac{1}{3}, x = -6$

## Graphing quadratic functions in vertex form

1)

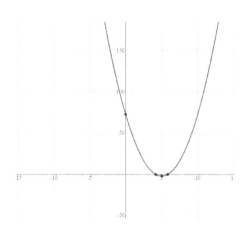

2)

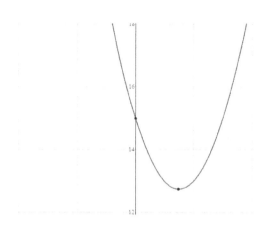

## Solve quadratic inequalities

1) $-5 < x < -2$

2) $x < -5 \; or \; x > -4$

3) $x < 4 \; or \; x > 4$

4) $2 \le x \le 6$

5) $5 \le x \le 6$

6) $x \le 3 \; or \; x \ge 9$

7) $all \; real \; numbers$

8) $-6 \le x \le 6$

9) $x \le 4 \; or \; x \ge 9$

10) $-12 \le x \le -3$

11) $x < -1 \; or \; x > 3$

12) $1 < x < 2$

## Graphing quadratic inequalities

1)

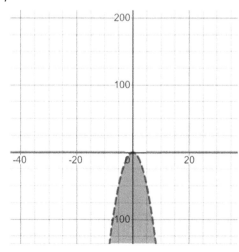

2)

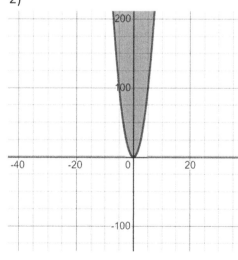

# Chapter 4:
# Complex Numbers

**Math Topics that you'll learn in this chapter:**

✓ Adding and Subtracting Complex Numbers

✓ Multiplying and Dividing Complex Numbers

✓ Rationalizing Imaginary Denominators

*Mathematics is a hard thing to love. It has the unfortunate habit, like a rude dog, of turning its most unfavorable side towards you when you first make contact with it. ~ David Whiteland*

# Adding and Subtracting Complex Numbers

**Step-by-step guide:**

- ✓ A complex number is expressed in the form $a + bi$, where $a$ and $b$ are real numbers, and $i$, which is called an imaginary number, is a solution of the equation $x^2 = -1$
- ✓ For adding complex numbers: $(a + bi) + (c + di) = (a + c) + (b + d)i$
- ✓ For subtracting complex numbers: $(a + bi) - (c + di) = (a - c) + (b - d)i$

## Examples:

1) Solve: $10 + (-5 - 3i) - 2$

   Remove parentheses: $10 + (-5 - 3i) - 2 \rightarrow 10 - 5 - 3i - 2$

   Combine like terms: $10 - 5 - 3i - 2 = 3 - 3i$

2) Solve: $-3 + (4i) + (9 - 2i)$

   Remove parentheses: $-3 + (4i) + (9 - 2i) \rightarrow -3 + 4i + 9 - 2i$

   Group like terms: $-3 + 4i + 9 - 2i \rightarrow 6 + 2i$

## ✏ *Simplify.*

1) $(1 - 2i) + (-4i) =$

2) $12 + (2 - 6i) =$

3) $-5 + (-2 - 8i) =$

4) $(-4i) - (7 - 2i) =$

5) $(-3 - 2i) - (2i) =$

6) $(8 - 6i) + (-5i) =$

7) $(-3 + 6i) - (-9 - i) =$

8) $(-5 + 15i) - (-3 + 3i) =$

9) $(-14 + i) - (-12 - 11i) =$

10) $(-18 - 3i) + (11 + 5i) =$

11) $(-11 - 9i) - (-9 - 3i) =$

12) $-8 + (2i) + (-8 + 6i) =$

# Multiplying and Dividing Complex Numbers

**Step-by-step guide:**

- ✓ Multiplying complex numbers: $(a + bi) + (c + di) = (ac - bd) + (ad + bc)i$

- ✓ Dividing complex numbers: $\dfrac{a+bi}{c+di} = \dfrac{a+bi}{c+di} \times \dfrac{c-di}{c-di} = \dfrac{ac+b}{c^2-d^2} + \dfrac{bc+ad}{c^2-d^2}i$

- ✓ Imaginary number rule: $i^2 = -1$

## Examples:

1) Solve: $\dfrac{4-2i}{2+i} =$

   Use the rule for dividing complex numbers:
   $$\frac{a+bi}{c+di} = \frac{a+bi}{c+di} \times \frac{c-di}{c-di} = \frac{ac+bd}{c^2-d^2} + \frac{bc+ad}{c^2-d^2}i \to$$
   $$\frac{4-2i}{2+i} \times \frac{2-i}{2-i} = \frac{(4 \times (2)) + (-2)(1)}{2^2 + (1)^2} + \frac{(-2 \times (2)) - (4)(1)}{2^2 + (1)^2}i = \frac{6-8i}{5} = \frac{6}{5} - \frac{8}{5}i$$

2) Solve: $(2 - 3i)(4 - 3i)$

   Use the rule: $(a + bi) + (c + di) = (ac - bd) + (ad + bc)i$

   $(2.4 - (-3)(-3)) + (2(-3) + (-3).4)i = -1 - 18i$

## ✎ Simplify.

1) $(-2 - i)(4 + i) =$

2) $(2 - 2i)^2 =$

3) $(4 - 3i)(6 - 6i) =$

4) $(5 + 4i)^2 =$

5) $(4i)(-i)(2 - 5i) =$

6) $(2 - 8i)(3 - 5i) =$

7) $\dfrac{9i}{3-i} =$

8) $\dfrac{2+4i}{14+4i} =$

9) $\dfrac{5+6i}{-1+8i} =$

10) $\dfrac{-8-i}{-4-6i} =$

11) $\dfrac{-1+5i}{-8-7i} =$

12) $\dfrac{-2-9i}{-2+7i} =$

# Rationalizing Imaginary Denominators

**Step-by-step guide:**

- ✓ Step 1: Find the conjugate (it's the denominator with different sign between the two terms.
- ✓ Step 2: Multiply numerator and denominator by the conjugate.
- ✓ Step 3: Simplify if needed.

## Examples:

1) Solve: $\dfrac{2-3i}{6i}$

Multiply by the conjugate: $\dfrac{-i}{-i} \cdot \dfrac{2-3i}{6i} = \dfrac{(2-3i)(-i)}{6i(-i)} = \dfrac{-3-2i}{6} = -\dfrac{1}{2} - \dfrac{1}{3}i$

2) Solve: $\dfrac{8i}{2-4i}$

Factor $2 - 4i = 2(1-2i)$, then: $\dfrac{8i}{2(1-2i)} = \dfrac{4i}{(1-2i)}$

Multiply by the conjugate $\dfrac{1+2i}{1+2i}$: $\dfrac{4i(1+2i)}{(1-2i)(1+2i)} = \dfrac{-8+4i}{5} = -\dfrac{8}{5} + \dfrac{4}{5}i$

## ✍ *Simplify.*

1) $\dfrac{-8}{-5i} =$

2) $\dfrac{-5}{-i} =$

3) $\dfrac{3}{5i} =$

4) $\dfrac{6}{-4i} =$

5) $\dfrac{-6-i}{-1+6i} =$

6) $\dfrac{-9-3i}{-3+3i} =$

7) $\dfrac{4i+1}{-1+3i} =$

8) $\dfrac{6-3i}{2-i} =$

9) $\dfrac{-5+2i}{2-3i} =$

10) $\dfrac{-9-i}{2-i} =$

11) $\dfrac{-10-5i}{-6+6i} =$

12) $\dfrac{-5-9i}{9+8i} =$

# Answers – Chapter 4

## Adding and subtracting complex numbers

1)  $1 - 6i$
2)  $14 - 6i$
3)  $-7 - 8i$
4)  $-7 - 2i$

5)  $-3 - 4i$
6)  $8 - 11i$
7)  $6 + 7i$
8)  $-2 + 12i$

9)  $-2 + 12i$
10) $-7 + 2i$
11) $-2 - 6i$
12) $-16 + 8i$

## Multiplying and dividing complex numbers

1)  $-7 - 6i$
2)  $-8i$
3)  $6 - 42i$
4)  $9 + 40i$
5)  $8 - 20i$
6)  $-34 - 34i$

7)  $-\frac{9}{10} + \frac{27}{10}i$
8)  $\frac{11}{53} + \frac{12}{53}i$
9)  $\frac{43}{65} - \frac{46}{65}i$

10) $\frac{19}{26} + \frac{11}{13}i$
11) $-\frac{27}{113} - \frac{47}{113}i$
12) $-\frac{59}{53} + \frac{32}{53}i$

## Rationalizing imaginary denominators

1)  $\frac{-8}{5}i$
2)  $-5i$
3)  $-\frac{3}{5}i$
4)  $\frac{3}{2}i$
5)  $i$
6)  $1 + 2i$
7)  $\frac{11}{10} - \frac{7}{10}i$
8)  $3$

9)  $-\frac{16}{13} - \frac{11}{13}i$
10) $-\frac{17}{5} + \frac{11}{5}i$
11) $\frac{5}{12} + \frac{5}{4}i$
12) $-\frac{117}{145} - \frac{41}{145}i$

# Chapter 5:
# Polynomial Operations

**Math Topics that you'll learn in this chapter:**

- ✓ Writing Polynomials in Standard Form

- ✓ Simplifying Polynomials

- ✓ Adding and Subtracting Polynomials

- ✓ Multiplying Monomials

- ✓ Multiplying and Dividing Monomials

- ✓ Multiplying a Polynomial and a Monomial

- ✓ Multiplying Binomials

- ✓ Factoring Trinomials

- ✓ Operations with Polynomials

*Mathematics is the supreme judge; from its decisions there is no appeal. - Tobias Dantzig*

# Writing Polynomials in Standard Form

**Step-by-step guide:**

✓ A polynomial function $f(x)$ of degree $n$ is of the form
$$f(x) = a_n x^n + a_{n-1} x_{n-1} + \cdots + a_1 x + a_0$$

✓ The first term is the one with the biggest power!

*Example:*

1) Write this polynomial in standard form. $8 + 5x^2 - 3x^3 =$

   The first term is the one with the biggest power: $8 + 5x^2 - 3x^3 = -3x^3 + 5x^2 + 8$

2) Write this polynomial in standard form. $5x^2 - 9x^5 + 8x^3 - 11 =$

   The first term is the one with the biggest power: $5x^2 - 9x^5 + 8x^3 - 11 =$
   $-9x^5 + 8x^3 + 5x^2 - 11$

✑ *Write each polynomial in standard form.*

1) $2x - 5x =$

2) $5 + 12x - 8x =$

3) $x^2 - 2x^3 + 1 =$

4) $2 + 2x^2 - 1 =$

5) $-x^2 + 4x - 2x^3 =$

6) $-2x^2 + 2x^3 + 12 =$

7) $18 - 5x + 9x^4 =$

8) $2x^2 + 13x - 2x^3 =$

9) $8 + 4x^2 - x^3 =$

10) $2x + 3x^3 - 2x^2 =$

11) $-4x^2 + 4x - 6x^3 =$

12) $-3x^2 + 2 - 5x =$

# Simplifying Polynomials

**Step-by-step guide:**

✓ Find "like" terms. (they have same variables with same power).

✓ Use "FOIL". (First–Out–In–Last) for binomials:

$$(x + a)(x + b) = x^2 + (b + a)x + ab$$

✓ Add or Subtract "like" terms using order of operation.

*Example:*

1) Simplify this expression. $2x(2x - 4) =$

Use Distributive Property: $2x(2x - 4) = 4x^2 - 8x$

2) Simplify this expression. $(x + 2)(x - 5) =$

First apply FOIL method: $(a + b)(c + d) = ac + ad + bc + bd$

$(x + 2)(x - 5) = x^2 - 5x + 2x - 10$

Now combine like terms: $x^2 - 5x + 2x - 10 = x^2 - 3x - 10$

✎ *Simplify each expression.*

1) $2(4x - 6) =$

2) $5(3x - 4) =$

3) $x(2x - 5) =$

4) $4(5x + 3) =$

5) $2x(6x - 2) =$

6) $x(3x + 8) =$

7) $(x - 2)(x + 4) =$

8) $(x + 3)(x + 2) =$

9) $(x - 4)(x - 7) =$

10) $(2x + 4)(2x - 5) =$

11) $(4x - 3)(x - 6) =$

12) $(3x + 5)(2x + 4) =$

# Adding and Subtracting Polynomials

**Step-by-step guide:**

✓ Adding polynomials is just a matter of combining like terms, with some order of operations considerations thrown in.
✓ Be careful with the minus signs, and don't confuse addition and multiplication!

*Example:*

1) **Simplify the expressions.** $(2x^3 - 4x^4) - (2x^4 - 6x^3) =$

First use Distributive Property for $-(2x^4 - 6x^3) = -2x^4 + 6x^3$

$(2x^3 - 4x^4) - (2x^4 - 6x^3) = 2x^3 - 4x^4 - 2x^4 + 6x^3$

Now combine like terms: $2x^3 - 4x^4 - 2x^4 + 6x^3 = -6x^4 + 8x^3$

2) **Add expressions.** $(x^3 - 2) + (5x^3 - 3x^2) =$

Remove parentheses: $(x^3 - 2) + (5x^3 - 3x^2) = x^3 - 2 + 5x^3 - 3x^2$

Now combine like terms: $x^3 - 2 + 5x^3 - 3x^2 = 6x^3 - 3x^2 - 2$

✎ *Add or subtract expressions.*

1) $(x^2 - x) + (3x^2 - 5x) =$

2) $(x^3 + 2x) - (3x^3 + 2) =$

3) $(2x^3 - 4) + (2x^3 - 2) =$

4) $(-x^2 - 2) + (2x^2 + 1) =$

5) $(4x^2 + 3) - (3 - 3x^2) =$

6) $(x^3 + 3x^2) - (x^3 - 8) =$

7) $(7x - 9) + (3x + 5) =$

8) $(x^4 - 2x) - (x - x^4) =$

9) $(2x - 4x^3) - (2x^3 + 3x) =$

10) $(x^3 + 5) - (5 - 2x^3) =$

11) $(3x^2 + 2x^3) - (4x^3 + 5) =$

12) $(6x^2 - x) + (2x - 5x^2) =$

# Multiplying Monomials

**Step-by-step guide:**

✓ A monomial is a polynomial with just one term, like $2x$ or $7y$.

*Example:*

1) ***Multiply expressions.*** $-2xy^4z^2 \times 4x^2y^5z^3 =$

Use this formula: $x^a \times x^b = x^{a+b}$

$x \times x^2 = x^{1+2} = x^3$ , $y^4 \times y^5 = y^{4+5} = y^9$ and $z^2 \times z^3 = z^{2+3} = z^5$

Then: $-2xy^4z^2 \times 4x^2y^5z^3 = -8x^3y^9z^5$

2) ***Multiply expressions.*** $-4a^4b^3 \times 5a^3b^2 =$

Use this formula: $x^a \times x^b = x^{a+b}$

$a^4 \times a^3 = a^{4+3} = a^7$ and $b^3 \times b^2 = b^{3+2} = b^5$

Then: $-4a^4b^3 \times 5a^3b^2 = -20a^7b^5$

✎ *Simplify each expression.*

1) $(-2x^4) \times (-5x^3) =$

2) $8x^8 \times -2x^2 =$

3) $5xy^4 \times 2x^2 =$

4) $-2x^6y \times 8xy =$

5) $3x^5 \times (-4x^3y^5) =$

6) $9x^3y^2 \times 3x^2y =$

7) $7xy^4 \times 8x^3y^5 =$

8) $(-5x^2y^4) \times (-2xy^3) =$

9) $9x^5y^2 \times 5x^6y^3 =$

10) $12x^5y^2 \times 2x^3y^3 =$

11) $11x^4y^3z \times 3x^5z^2 =$

12) $20x^5y^8 \times 3x^2y^4 =$

# Multiplying and Dividing Monomials

**Step-by-step guide:**

✓ When you divide two monomials you need to divide their coefficients and then divide their variables.
✓ In case of exponents with the same base, you need to subtract their powers.
✓ Exponent's rules:

$$x^a \times x^b = x^{a+b}, \qquad \frac{x^a}{x^b} = x^{a-b}$$
$$\frac{1}{x^b} = x^{-b}, \quad (x^a)^b = x^{a \times b}$$
$$(xy)^a = x^a \times y^a$$

*Example:*

1) **Multiply expressions.** $(8x^5)(-2x^4) =$
   Use this formula: $x^a \times x^b = x^{a+b} \rightarrow x^5 \times x^4 = x^9$
   Then: $(8x^5)(-2x^4) = -16x^9$

2) **Dividing expressions.** $\frac{-12x^4y^3}{2xy^2} =$
   Use this formula: $\frac{x^a}{x^b} = x^{a-b}$ , $\frac{x^4}{x} = x^{4-1} = x^3$ and $\frac{y^3}{y^2} = y$
   Then: $\frac{-12x^4y^3}{2xy^2} = -6x^3y$

✍ *Simplify each expression.*

1) $(x^2y)(xy^2) =$

2) $(x^4y^2)(2x^5y) =$

3) $(-2x^2y)(4x^4y^3) =$

4) $(-3x^5y^2)(2x^2y^4) =$

5) $(-4x^5y^3)(-2x^3y^4) =$

6) $(6x^6y^5)(3x^3y^8) =$

7) $\frac{-2x^4y^3}{x^2y^2} =$

8) $\frac{8x^4y^7}{2x^3y^4} =$

9) $\frac{25\ ^6y^5}{5x^3y^2} =$

10) $\frac{18x^{12}y^{14}}{6x^8y^6} =$

11) $\frac{45\ ^{13}y^{15}}{9x^9y^4} =$

12) $\frac{-60x^{20}y^{16}}{3x^{11}y^{13}} =$

# Multiplying a Polynomial and a Monomial

**Step-by-step guide:**

- ✓ When multiplying monomials, use the product rule for exponents.
- ✓ When multiplying a monomial by a polynomial, use the distributive property.

$$a \times (b + c) = a \times b + a \times c$$

*Example:*

1) *Multiply expressions.* $2x(-2x + 4) =$

   Use Distributive Property: $2x(-2x + 4) = -4x^2 + 8x$

2) *Multiply expressions.* $-2x(3x^2 + 4y^2) =$

   Use Distributive Property: $-2x(3x^2 + 4y^2) = -6x^3 - 8xy^2$

✎ *Find each product.*

1) $-2x(5x + 2y) =$

2) $3x(2x - y) =$

3) $4x(x + 5y) =$

4) $-4x(6x - 3) =$

5) $x(-2x + 9y) =$

6) $2x(5x - 8y) =$

7) $x(2x + 4y - 3) =$

8) $2x(x^2 - 2y^2) =$

9) $-4x(2x + 4y) =$

10) $3(x^2 + 7y^2) =$

11) $4x(-x^2y + 2y) =$

12) $5(x^2 - 4xy + 6) =$

# Multiplying Binomials

**Step-by-step guide:**

✓ Use "FOIL". (First–Out–In–Last)
$$(x + a)(x + b) = x^2 + (b + a)x + ab$$

*Example:*

1) **Multiply Binomials.** $(x + 3)(x - 2) =$

Use "FOIL". (First–Out–In–Last): $(x + 3)(x - 2) = x^2 - 2x + 3x - 6$

Then simplify: $x^2 - 2x + 3x - 6 = x^2 + x - 6$

2) **Multiply Binomials.** $(x - 4)(x - 2) =$

Use "FOIL". (First–Out–In–Last):

$(x - 4)(x - 2) = x^2 - 2x - 4x + 8$

Then simplify: $x^2 - 6x + 8 =$

✍ *Find each product.*

1) $(x - 2)(x + 4) =$

2) $(x + 5)(x - 2) =$

3) $(x - 3)(x - 4) =$

4) $(x + 2)(x + 2) =$

5) $(x - 6)(x - 3) =$

6) $(x + 5)(x + 7) =$

7) $(x + 2)(x - 8) =$

8) $(x - 9)(x + 4) =$

9) $(x + 5)(x + 6) =$

10) $(x - 8)(x + 3) =$

11) $(x + 5)(x + 5) =$

12) $(x + 7)(x + 4) =$

# Factoring Trinomials

**Step-by-step guide:**

- ✓ "FOIL":
$$(x + a)(x + b) = x^2 + (b + a)x + ab$$
- ✓ "Difference of Squares":
$$a^2 - b^2 = (a + b)(a - b)$$
$$a^2 + 2ab + b^2 = (a + b)(a + b)$$
$$a^2 - 2ab + b^2 = (a - b)(a - b)$$
- ✓ "Reverse FOIL":
$$x^2 + (b + a)x + ab = (x + a)(x + b)$$

*Example:*

1) **Factor this trinomial.** $x^2 - 3x - 18 =$
   Break the expression into groups: $(x^2 + 3x) + (-6x - 18)$
   Now factor out $x$ from $x^2 + 3x : x(x + 2)$ , and factor out $-6$ from $-6x + 18: -6(x + 3)$
   Then: $= x(x + 3) - 6(x + 3)$ , now factor out like term: $x + 3$
   Then: $(x + 3)(x - 6)$

2) **Factor this trinomial.** $x^2 + x - 20 =$
   Break the expression into groups: $(x^2 - 4x) + (5x - 20)$
   Now factor out $x$ from $x^2 - 4x : x(x + 3)$ , and factor out 5 from $6x - 18: 5(x - 4)$
   Then: $= x(x - 4) + 5(x - 4)$ , now factor out like term: $x - 4$
   Then: $(x + 5)(x - 4)$

✎ *Factor each trinomial.*

1) $x^2 + 3x - 10 =$

2) $x^2 - x - 6 =$

3) $x^2 + 8x + 15 =$

4) $x^2 - 7x + 12 =$

5) $x^2 - x - 20 =$

6) $x^2 + 11x + 18 =$

7) $x^2 + 3x - 28 =$

8) $x^2 - 2x - 48 =$

9) $x^2 - 13x + 36 =$

10) $x^2 - x - 56 =$

11) $x^2 - 4x - 45 =$

12) $x^2 - 8x - 48 =$

# Operations with Polynomials

**Step-by-step guide:**

✓ When multiplying a monomial by a polynomial, use the distributive property.

$$a \times (b + c) = a \times b + a \times c$$

*Example:*

1) *Multiply.* $4(3x - 5) =$

Use the distributive property: $4(3x - 5) = 12x - 20$

2) *Multiply.* $6x(3x + 7) =$

Use the distributive property: $6x(3x + 7) = 18x^2 + 42x$

✍ *Find each product.*

1) $2(3x + 2) =$

2) $-3(2x + 5) =$

3) $4(7x - 3) =$

4) $5(2x - 4) =$

5) $3x(2x - 7) =$

6) $x^2(3x + 4) =$

7) $x^3(x + 5) =$

8) $x^4 (5x - 3) =$

9) $4(2x^2 + 3x - 2) =$

10) $-2(x^2 - 6x + 5) =$

11) $5(2x^2 + 4x - 6) =$

12) $-x(3x^2 + 7x + 5) =$

# Answers – Chapter 5

## Writing Polynomials in Standard Form

1) $-3x$
2) $4x + 5$
3) $-2x^3 + x^2 + 1$
4) $2x^2 + 1$

5) $-2x^3 - x^2 + 4x$
6) $2x^3 - 2x^2 + 12$
7) $9x^4 - 5x + 18$
8) $-2x^3 + 2x^2 + 13x$

9) $-x^3 + 4x^2 + 8$
10) $3x^3 - 2x^2 + 2x$
11) $-6x^3 - 4x^2 + 4x$
12) $-3x^2 - 5x + 2$

## Simplifying Polynomials

1) $8x - 12$
2) $15x - 20$
3) $2x^2 - 5x$
4) $20x + 12$

5) $12x^2 - 4x$
6) $3x^2 + 8x$
7) $x^2 + 2x - 8$
8) $x^2 + 5x + 6$

9) $x^2 - 11x + 28$
10) $4x^2 - 2x - 20$
11) $4x^2 - 27x + 18$
12) $6x^2 + 22x + 20$

## Adding and Subtracting Polynomials

1) $4x^2 - 6x$
2) $-2x^3 + 2x - 2$
3) $4x^3 - 6$
4) $x^2 - 1$

5) $7x^2$
6) $3x^2 + 8$
7) $10x - 4$
8) $2x^4 - 3x$

9) $-6x^3 - 3x$
10) $3x^3$
11) $-2x^3 + 3x^2 - 5$
12) $x^2 + x$

## Multiplying Monomials

1) $10x^7$
2) $-16x^{10}$
3) $10x^3y^4$
4) $-16x^7y^2$

5) $-12x^8y^5$
6) $27x^5y^3$
7) $56x^4y^9$
8) $10x^3y^7$

9) $45x^{11}y^5$
10) $24x^8y^5$
11) $33x^9y^3z^3$
12) $60x^7y^{12}$

## Multiplying and Dividing Monomials

1) $x^3 y^3$
2) $2x^9 y^3$
3) $-8x^6 y^4$
4) $-6x^7 y^6$

5) $8x^8 y^7$
6) $18x^9 y^{13}$
7) $-2x^2 y$
8) $4xy^3$

9) $5x^3 y^3$
10) $3x^4 y^8$
11) $5x^4 y^{11}$
12) $-20x^9 y^3$

## Multiplying a Polynomial and a Monomial

1) $-10x^2 - 4xy$
2) $6x^2 - 3xy$
3) $4x^2 + 20xy$
4) $-24x^2 + 12x$

5) $-2x^2 + 9xy$
6) $10x^2 - 16xy$
7) $2x^2 + 4xy - 3x$
8) $2x^3 - 4xy^2$

9) $-8x^2 - 16xy$
10) $3x^2 + 21y^2$
11) $-4x^3 y + 8xy$
12) $5x^2 - 20xy + 30$

## Multiplying Binomials

1) $x^2 + 2x - 8$
2) $x^2 + 3x - 10$
3) $x^2 - 7x + 12$
4) $x^2 + 4x + 4$

5) $x^2 - 9x + 18$
6) $x^2 + 12x + 35$
7) $x^2 - 6x - 16$
8) $x^2 - 5x - 36$

9) $x^2 + 11x + 30$
10) $x^2 - 5x - 24$
11) $x^2 + 10x + 25$
12) $x^2 + 11x + 28$

## Factoring Trinomials

1) $(x - 2)(x + 5)$
2) $(x + 2)(x - 3)$
3) $(x + 5)(x + 3)$
4) $(x - 3)(x - 4)$
5) $(x - 5)(x + 4)$

6) $(x + 2)(x + 9)$
7) $(x + 7)(x - 4)$
8) $(x - 8)(x + 6)$
9) $(x - 4)(x - 9)$
10) $(x - 8)(x +$

7)
11) $(x - 9)(x + 5)$
12) $(x + 4)(x -$
12)

## Operations with Polynomials

1) $6x + 4$
2) $-6x - 15$
3) $28x - 12$
4) $10x - 20$
5) $6x^2 - 21x$
6) $3x^3 + 4x^2$

7) $x^4 + 5x^3$
8) $5x^5 - 3x^4$
9) $8x^2 + 12x - 8$
10) $-2x^2 + 12x - 10$
11) $10x^2 + 20x - 30$
12) $-3x^3 - 7x^2 - 5x$

# Chapter 6:
# Functions Operations

**Math Topics that you'll learn in this chapter:**

- ✓ Function Notation

- ✓ Adding and Subtracting Functions

- ✓ Multiplying and Dividing Functions

- ✓ Composition of Functions

*"The mathematician does not study pure mathematics because it is useful: he studies it because he delights in it and he*

*delights in it because it is beautiful" Georg Cantor*

# Function Notation

**Step-by-step guide:**

- ✓ Functions are mathematical operations that assign unique outputs to given inputs.
- ✓ Function notation is the way a function is written. It is meant to be a precise way of giving information about the function without a rather lengthy written explanation.
- ✓ The most popular function notation is $f(x)$ which is read "$f$ of $x$".

## *Examples:*

1) Evaluate: $h(n) = n^2 - 2$, find $h(4)$. Substitute $x$ with 4:

Then: $h(n) = n^2 - 2 \rightarrow h(4) = (4)^2 - 2 \rightarrow h(4) = 16 - 2 \rightarrow h(4) = 14$

2) Evaluate: $w(x) = 4x - 1$, find $w(2)$. Substitute $x$ with 4: Then: $w(x) = 4x - 1 \rightarrow w(2) = 4(2) - 1 \rightarrow w(2) = 8 - 1 \rightarrow w(2) = 7$

## ✍ *Evaluate each function.*

1) $f(x) = 2x + 8$, find $f(-1)$

2) $g(n) = n + 12$, find $g(2)$

3) $g(n) = -2n + 3$, find $g(-2)$

4) $h(n) = -2n^2 - 6n$, find $h(-1)$

5) $g(a) = 3a^2 + 2a$, find $g(3)$

6) $h(x) = x^2 + 1$, find $h(-2)$

7) $h(x) = x^3 + 8$, find $h(-1)$

8) $h(x) = 2x^2 - 10$, find $h(4)$

9) $h(a) = -2a - 5$, find $h(3)$

10) $k(a) = -7a + 3$, find $k(-2)$

11) $h(x) = 4x + 5$, find $h(6)$

12) $h(n) = -n^2 - 10$, find $h(5)$

# Adding and Subtracting Functions

**Step-by-step guide:**

✓ Just like we can add and subtract numbers, we can add and subtract functions. For example, if we had functions f and g, we could create two new functions:

✓ f + g and f - g.

## Examples:

1) $g(a) = a - 1$, $f(a) = a + 5$, **Find:** $(g + f)(-1)$

   $(g + f)(a) = g(a) + f(a)$, Then: $(g + f)(a) = a - 1 + a + 5 = 2a + 4$

   Substitute $a$ with $-1$: $(g + f)(a) = 2a + 4 = 2(-1) + 4 = -2 + 4 = 2$

2) $f(x) = 3x - 3$, $g(x) = x - 5$, **Find:** $(f - g)(3)$

   $(f - g)(x) = f(x) - g(x)$, then: $(f - g)(x) = 3x - 3 - (x - 5) = 3x - 3 - x + 5$

   $$= 2x + 2$$

   Substitute $x$ with 3: $(f - g)(1) = 2(3) + 2 = 8$

## ✎ *Perform the indicated operation.*

1) $g(x) = x + 2$

   $h(x) = 2x + 3$

   Find: $g(-1) - h(-1)$

2) $h(x) = 2x + 1$

   $g(x) = -x + 4$

   Find: $(h + g)(2)$

3) $f(x) = 2x^2 - 1$

   $g(x) = x^2 + 2$

   Find: $(f - g)(-1)$

4) $h(n) = -n^2 + 3$

   $g(n) = -n + 9$

   Find: $(h - g)(3)$

5) $g(x) = x^2 - 1$

   $f(x) = 2x + 12$

   Find: $(g - f)(2)$

6) $g(x) = 2x^3 + 8$

   $f(x) = -2x^2 - 10$

   Find: $(g + f)(2)$

# Multiplying and Dividing Functions

**Step-by-step guide:**

    ✓ Just like we can multiply and divide numbers, we can multiply and divide functions. For example, if we had functions f and g, we could create two new functions: f × g, and $\frac{f}{g}$.

## *Examples:*

1) $g(x) = x + 1, f(x) = x - 2,$ Find: $(g.f)(2)$

    $(g.f)(x) = g(x).f(x) = (x + 1)(x - 2) = x^2 - 2x + x - 2 = x^2 - x - 2$

    Substitute $x$ with 2:

    $(g.f)(x) = x^2 - x - 2 = (2)^2 - 2 - 2 = 4 - 2 - 2 = 0$

2) $f(x) = x - 2, h(x) = x + 8,$ Find: $\left(\frac{f}{h}\right)(-1)$

    $\left(\frac{f}{h}\right)(x) = \frac{f(x)}{h(x)} = \frac{x-2}{x+8}$

    Substitute $x$ with $-1$: $\left(\frac{f}{h}\right)(x) = \frac{x-2}{x+8} = \frac{(-1)-2}{(-1)+8} = \frac{-3}{7} = -\frac{3}{7}$

✎ *Perform the indicated operation.*

1) $f(x) = x - 1$

    $g(x) = x + 4$

    Find $(\frac{f}{g})(2)$

2) $g(a) = 2a + 6$

    $f(a) = a - 12$

    Find $(\frac{g}{f})(4)$

3) $g(x) = 2x + 4$

    $h(x) = x - 3$

    Find $(g.h)(-1)$

4) $g(n) = n^2 + 6$

    $h(n) = 2n - 8$

    Find $(g.h)(2)$

5) $f(x) = x^2 - 2$

    $g(x) = x + 1$

    Find $(f.g)(2)$

6) $f(x) = 2a^2 + 4$

    $g(x) = 6 + 2a$

    Find $(\frac{f}{g})(2)$

# Composition of Functions

**Step-by-step guide:**

- ✓ The term "composition of functions" (or "composite function") refers to the combining together of two or more functions in a manner where the output from one function becomes the input for the next function.
- ✓ The notation used for composition is: $(f \circ g)(x) = f(g(x))$

## *Examples:*

**1)** *Using* $f(x) = x - 2$ *and* $g(x) = x$, *find:* $f(g(2))$

$(f \circ g)(x) = f(g(x))$

*Then:* $(f \circ g)(x) = f\big(g(x)\big) = f(x) = x - 2$

Substitute $x$ with 2: $(f \circ g)(2) = 2 - 2 = 0$

**2)** *Using* $f(x) = x + 8$ *and* $g(x) = x - 2$, *find:* $g(f(4))$

$(f \circ g)(x) = f(g(x))$

*Then:* $(g \circ f)(x) = g\big(f(x)\big) = g(x + 8)$, *now substitute* $x$ *in* f(x) *by* $x + 8$. **Then:**
$g(x + 8) = (x + 8) - 2 = x + 8 - 2 = x + 6$

Substitute $x$ with 4: $(g \circ f)(4) = g\big(f(x)\big) = 4 + 6 = 10$

✎ *Using* $f(x) = x + 2$ *and* $g(x) = x - 1$, *find:*

1) $f(g(1))$            3) $g(f(-1))$

2) $f(f(-2))$           4) $g(g(2))$

✎ *Using* $f(x) = 5x + 2$ *and* $g(x) = x - 6$, *find:*

5) $f(g(-1))$          7) $g(f(-2))$

6) $f(f(2))$            8) $g(g(5))$

# Answers – Chapter 6

## Function Notation

1) 6
2) 14
3) 7
4) 4
5) 33
6) 5

7) 7
8) 22
9) $-11$
10) $-11$
11) 29
12) $-35$

## Adding and Subtracting Functions

1) 0
2) 7
3) $-13$

4) $-2$
5) $-12$
6) 6

## Multiplying and Dividing Functions

1) $\frac{1}{6}$

2) $-8$

3) 6

4) $-\frac{7}{4}$

5) $-40$

6) $\frac{6}{5}$

## Composition of functions

1) 2

2) 2

3) 0

4) 0

5) $-33$

6) 62

7) $-14$

8) $-7$

# Chapter 7: Logarithms

## Topics that you'll learn in this chapter:

- ✓ Evaluating Logarithms
- ✓ Properties of Logarithms
- ✓ Natural Logarithms
- ✓ Solving Logarithmic Equations

*The study of mathematics, like the Nile, begins in minuteness but ends in magnificence.*"

*- Charles Caleb Colton*

# Evaluating Logarithms

**Step-by-step guide:**

✓ Logarithm is another way of writing exponent. $log_b\, y = x$ is equivalent to $y = b^x$

✓ Learn some logarithms rules:

$$log_b\,(x) = \frac{log_d\,(x)}{log_d\,(b)} \qquad\qquad log_a\, x^b = b\, log_a\, x$$

$$log_a\, a = 1 \qquad\qquad\qquad\qquad log_a\, 1 = 0$$

## Examples:

1) **Evaluate:** $log_2\, 16$

Rewrite 16 in power base form: $16 = 2^4$, then: $log_2\, 16 = log_2(2^4)$

Use log rule: $log_a(x^b) = b.\, log_a(x) \rightarrow log_2(2^4) = 4log_2(2)$

Use log rule: $log_a(a) = 1 \rightarrow log_2(2) = 1.\quad 4log_2(2) = 4 \times 1 = 4$

2) **Evaluate:** $log_6\, 216$

Rewrite 216 in power base form: $216 = 6^3$, then: $log_6\, 216 = log_6(6^3)$

Use log rule: $log_a(x^b) = b.\, log_a(x) \rightarrow log_6(6^3) = 3log_6(6)$

Use log rule: $log_a(a) = 1 \rightarrow log_6(6) = 1.\quad 3log_6(6) = 3 \times 1 = 3$

✍ *Evaluate each logarithm.*

1) $log_2\, 8 =$ 

3) $log_4\, 256 =$

2) $log_2\, \frac{1}{32} =$ 

4) $log_3\, \frac{1}{81} =$

✍ *Circle the points which are on the graph of the given logarithmic functions.*

5) $y = 2log_3(x + 1) + 2 \qquad (2, 4), \qquad (8, 4), \qquad (0, 3)$

6) $y = 3log_3(3x) - 2 \qquad (3, 6), \qquad (3, 4), \qquad (\frac{1}{3}, 2)$

7) $y = -2log_2 2(x - 1) + 1 \qquad (3, -3), \qquad (2, 1), \qquad (5, 5)$

8) $y = 4log_4(4x) + 7 \qquad (1, 7), \qquad (1, 11), \qquad (4, 8)$

# Properties of Logarithms

**Step-by-step guide:**

✓ Learn some logarithms properties:

$a^{log_a b} = b$

$log_a 1 = 0$

$log_a a = 1$

$log_a(x \cdot y) = log_a x + log_a y$

$log_a \frac{x}{y} = log_a x - log_a y$

$log_a \frac{1}{x} = - log_a x$

$log_a x^p = p \ log_a x$

$log_{x^k} x = \frac{1}{x} \ log_a x, for \ k \ \neq \ 0$

$log_a x = log_{a^c} x^c$

$log_a x = \frac{1}{log_x a}$

## Examples:

1) **Expand this logarithm.** $log \ (2 \times 3) =$

Use log rule: $log_a(x \cdot y) = log_a x + log_a y$

Then: $log \ (2 \times 3) = log2 + log3$

2) Condense this expression to a single logarithm. $log \ 4 - log \ 3 =$

Use log rule: $log_a x - log_a y = log_a \frac{x}{y}$

Then: $log \ 4 - log \ 3 = log \frac{4}{3}$

✍ *Expand each logarithm.*

1) $log \ (\frac{1}{2}) =$

2) $log \ (\frac{3}{5}) =$

3) $log \ (\frac{1}{3})^2 \ =$

4) $log \ (8 \times 2^5) =$

5) $log \ (\frac{2}{7})^3 \ =$

6) $log \left( \frac{5^3}{9} \right) =$

✍ *Condense each expression to a single logarithm.*

7) $log \ 2 - \ log \ 5 =$

8) $2 \ log \ 3 - 2 \ log \ 4 =$

9) $4 \ log \ 3 - 4log \ 7 =$

10) $5 \ log \ 2 - \ 7log \ 9 =$

11) $log \ 12 - 6 \ log \ 4 =$

12) $3log \ 14 + 2log \ 18 =$

# Natural Logarithms

**Step-by-step guide:**

✓ A natural logarithm is a logarithm that has a special base of the mathematical constant e, which is an irrational number approximately equal to 2.71.

✓ The natural logarithm of $x$ is generally written as $ln\, x$, or $log_e x$.

**Examples:**

1) **Solve the equation for** x: $e^x = 5$

If $f(x) = g(x)$, then: $ln(f(x)) = ln(g(x)) \rightarrow ln(e^x) = ln(5)$

Use log rule: $log_a x^b = b\, log_a x \rightarrow ln(e^x) = x\, ln(e) \rightarrow xln(e) = ln(5)$

$ln(e) = 1$, then: $x = ln(5)$

2) **Solve equation for** x: $ln(5x - 1) = 1$

Use log rule: $a = log_b(b^a) \rightarrow 1 = ln(e^1) = ln(e) \rightarrow ln(5x - 1) = ln\,(e)$

When the logs have the same base: $log_b(f(x)) = log_b(g(x)) \rightarrow f(x) = g(x)$

$ln(5x - 1) = ln(e)$, then: $5x - 1 = e \rightarrow x = \frac{e+1}{5}$

✎ **Solve each equation for** x.

1)  $e^x = 2$

2)  $e^x = 4$

3)  $ln\, x = 8$

4)  $ln\,(ln\, x) = 3$

5)  $e^x = 27$

6)  $ln(3x + 2) = 8$

7)  $ln(9x - 1) = 1$

8)  $ln\, x = \frac{1}{4}$

✎ **Reduce the following expressions to simplest form.**

9) $e^{ln3+l} =$

10) $e^{ln\left(\frac{3}{e}\right)} =$

11)  $4\, ln(e^3) =$

12)  $ln(\frac{1}{e})^4 =$

# Solving Logarithmic Equations

**Step-by-step guide:**

- ✓ Convert the logarithmic equation to an exponential equation when it's possible. (If no base is indicated, the base of the logarithm is 10)
- ✓ Condense logarithms if you have more than one log on one side of the equation.
- ✓ Plug in the answers back into the original equation and check to see the solution works.

## Examples:

1) **Find the value of the variables in each equation.** $\log_2(25 - x^2) = 2$

   *Use log rule: $\log_b x = \log_b y$ then: $x = y$*

   $2 = \log_2(2^2)$, $\log_4(25 - x^2) = \log_2(2^2) = \log_2 4$

   Then: $25 - x^2 = 4 \to 25 - 16 = x^2 \to x^2 = 9 \to x = 3$

2) **Find the value of the variables in each equation.** $\log(8x + 3) = \log(2x - 6)$

   *When the logs have the same base: $f(x) = g(x)$, then: $\ln(f(x)) = \ln(g(x))$*

   $\log(8x + 3) = \log(2x - 6) \to 8x + 3 = 2x - 6 \to 8x + 3 - 2x + 6 = 0$

   $6x + 9 = 0 \to 6x = -9 \to x = \dfrac{-9}{6} = -\dfrac{3}{2}$

✎ *Find the value of the variables in each equation.*

1) $\log_5 8x = 0$

2) $\log_4 12x = 2$

3) $\log x + 2 = 1$

4) $\log x - \log 2 = 4$

5) $\log x + \log 8 = 2$

6) $\log 2 + \log x = 0$

7) $\log x + \log 6 = \log 36$

8) $2\log_2(x - 4) = 4$

9) $\log 3x = \log(x + 6)$

10) $\log(6x - 8) = \log(3x - 1)$

11) $\log(3x - 2) = \log(2x + 1)$

12) $-14 + \log_2(x + 1) = -10$

# Answers – Chapter 7

## *Evaluating logarithms*

1) 3
2) −5
3) 4

4) 4
5) (2, 4)
6) (3, 4)

7) (3, −3)
8) (1, 11)

## *Properties of logarithms*

1) $log\ 1 - log\ 2$
2) $log\ 3 - log\ 5$
3) $2\ log\ 1 - 2\ log\ 3$
4) $log\ 8 + 5\ log\ 2$
5) $3\log 2 - 3\log 7$
6) $3log5 - log\ 9$
7) $log\ \frac{2}{5}$

8) $log\ \frac{3^2}{4^2}$
9) $log\ \frac{3^4}{7^4}$
10) $log\ \frac{2^5}{9^7}$
11) $log\ \frac{12}{6^4}$
12) $log\ (14^3 18^2)$

## *Natural logarithms*

1) $x = ln\ 2$
2) $x = ln\ 4, x = 2ln\ (2)$
3) $x = e^8$
4) $x = e^{e^3}$

5) $x = ln\ 27, x = 3ln\ (3)$
6) $x = \frac{e^8 - 2}{3}$
7) $x = \frac{e+1}{9}$
8) $x = \sqrt[4]{e}$

9) 18
10) $\frac{3}{e}$
11) 12
12) −4

## *Solving logarithmic equations*

1) $\{\frac{1}{8}\}$
2) $\{\frac{4}{3}\}$
3) $\{\frac{1}{10}\}$

4) $x = 20,000$
5) $x = 800$
6) $x = 2$
7) $x = 6$
8) $x = 8$

9) $x = 3$
10) $x = \frac{7}{3}$
11) $x = 3$
12) $x = 15$

# Chapter 8:
# Radical Expressions

## Topics that you'll learn in this chapter:

- ✓ Simplifying Radical Expressions
- ✓ Simplifying Radical Expressions Involving Fractions
- ✓ Multiplying Radical Expressions
- ✓ Adding and Subtracting Radical Expressions
- ✓ Domain and Range of Radical Functions
- ✓ Radical Equations

*"Without mathematics, there's nothing you can do. Everything around you is mathematics. Everything around you is numbers." – Shakuntala Devi*

# Simplifying Radical Expressions

**Step-by-step guide:**

For square roots:

- ✓ Find the prime factors of the numbers inside the radical.
- ✓ Find the largest perfect score factor of the number.
- ✓ Rewrite the radical as the product of perfect score and its matching factor and simplify.

## *Examples:*

1) Find the square root of $\sqrt{169}$.
First factor the number: $169 = 13^2$, Then: $\sqrt{169} = \sqrt{13^2}$

Now use radical rule: $\sqrt[n]{a^n} = a$, Then: $\sqrt{13^2} = 13$

2) Evaluate. $\sqrt{9} \times \sqrt{25} =$
First factor the numbers: $9 = 3^2$ and $25 = 5^2$

Then: $\sqrt{9} \times \sqrt{25} = \sqrt{3^2} \times \sqrt{5^2}$

Now use radical rule: $\sqrt[n]{a^n} = a$, Then: $\sqrt{3^2} \times \sqrt{5^2} = 3 \times 5 = 15$

## ✎ *Simplify.*

1) $\sqrt{25x^2}$

2) $\sqrt{900x^2}$

3) $\sqrt{100x^2}$

4) $\sqrt{125a}$

5) $\sqrt{216v}$

6) $\sqrt{450x^2}$

7) $\sqrt{405}$

8) $\sqrt{512p^3}$

9) $\sqrt{216m^4}$

10) $\sqrt{264x^3y^3}$

11) $\sqrt{49x^3y^3}$

12) $\sqrt{16a^4b^3}$

## Simplifying Radical Expressions Involving Fractions

**Step-by-step guide:**

- ✓ Radical expressions cannot be in the denominator. (number in the bottom)
- ✓ To get rid of the radical in the denominator, multiply both numerator and denominator by the radical in the denominator.
- ✓ If there is a radical and another integer in the denominator, multiply both numerator and denominator by the conjugate of the denominator.
- ✓ The conjugate of a + b is a-b and vice versa.

## *Examples:*

1) *Simplify* $\frac{2}{\sqrt{3}-2}$

Multiply by the conjugate: $\frac{\sqrt{3}+2}{\sqrt{3}+2}$ $\rightarrow$ $\frac{2}{\sqrt{3}-2} \times \frac{\sqrt{3}+2}{\sqrt{3}+2}$

$(\sqrt{3}-2)(\sqrt{3}+2) = -1$ then: $\frac{2(\sqrt{3}+2)}{-1}$

Use the fraction rule: $\frac{a}{-b} = -\frac{a}{b} \rightarrow \frac{2(\sqrt{3}+2)}{-1} = -\frac{2(\sqrt{3}+2)}{1} = -2(\sqrt{3}+2)$

2) *Simplify* $\frac{3}{\sqrt{7}-2}$

Multiply by the conjugate: $\frac{\sqrt{7}+2}{\sqrt{7}+2}$

$\frac{3}{\sqrt{7}-2} \times \frac{\sqrt{7}+2}{\sqrt{7}+2} = \frac{3(\sqrt{7}+2)}{3} \rightarrow \frac{3(\sqrt{7}+2)}{3} = \sqrt{7}+2$

## ✎ *Simplify.*

1) $\frac{\sqrt{5m}}{\sqrt{m^3}}$

2) $\frac{8\sqrt{6}}{\sqrt{x}}$

3) $\frac{\sqrt{5}-\sqrt{3}}{\sqrt{3}-\sqrt{5}}$

4) $\frac{5\sqrt{3}-3\sqrt{2}}{3\sqrt{2}-2\sqrt{3}}$

5) $\frac{\sqrt{31x^5y^3}}{\sqrt{2xy^2}}$

6) $\frac{6\sqrt{45k^3}}{3\sqrt{5k}}$

7) $\frac{\sqrt{a}}{\sqrt{a}+\sqrt{b}}$

8) $\frac{2}{3+\sqrt{7}}$

9) $\frac{1+\sqrt{2}}{3+\sqrt{5}}$

10) $\frac{2+\sqrt{5}}{6-\sqrt{3}}$

11) $\frac{\sqrt{7}+\sqrt{5}}{\sqrt{5}+\sqrt{2}}$

12) $\frac{3\sqrt{2}-\sqrt{7}}{4\sqrt{2}+\sqrt{5}}$

# Multiplying Radical Expressions

**Step-by-step guide:**

- ✓ To multiply radical expressions:
- ✓ Multiply the numbers outside of the radicals.
- ✓ Multiply the numbers inside the radicals.
- ✓ Simplify if needed.

## *Examples:*

1) **Evaluate.** $\sqrt{16} \times \sqrt{9} =$

First factor the numbers: $16 = 4^2$ and $9 = 3^2$

Then: $\sqrt{16} \times \sqrt{9} = \sqrt{4^2} \times \sqrt{3^2}$

Now use radical rule: $\sqrt[n]{a^n} = a$, Then: $\sqrt{4^2} \times \sqrt{3^2} = 4 \times 3 = 12$

2) **Evaluate.** $2\sqrt{5} \times 3\sqrt{2} =$

Multiply the numbers: $2 \times 3 = 6$

$2\sqrt{5} \times 3\sqrt{2} = 6\sqrt{5}\sqrt{2}$

Use radical rule: $\sqrt{a}\sqrt{b} = \sqrt{ab} \rightarrow 6\sqrt{5}\sqrt{2} = 6\sqrt{5 \times 2} = 6\sqrt{10}$

✐ *Simplify.*

1) $\sqrt{4} \times 2\sqrt{9} =$

2) $2\sqrt{25} \times 3\sqrt{81} =$

3) $5\sqrt{49} \times 4\sqrt{16} =$

4) $2\sqrt{64} \times 7\sqrt{36} =$

5) $8\sqrt{16} \times 3\sqrt{100} =$

6) $-5\sqrt{12} \times -\sqrt{3} =$

7) $\sqrt{23a^2} \times \sqrt{23a} =$

8) $2\sqrt{20k^2} \times \sqrt{5k^2} =$

9) $\sqrt{12x^2} \times \sqrt{2x^3} =$

10) $12\sqrt{7x} \times \sqrt{5x^3} =$

11) $4\sqrt{9x^3} \times 7\sqrt{3x^2} =$

12) $3\sqrt{40x^5} \times 9\sqrt{2x} =$

# Adding and Subtracting Radical Expressions

**Step-by-step guide:**

- ✓ Only numbers that have the same radical part can be added or subtracted.
- ✓ Remember, combining "unlike" radical terms is not possible.
- ✓ For number with the same radical part, just add or subtract factors outside the radicals.

## *Examples:*

1) **Simplify** $4\sqrt{5} + 3\sqrt{5} =$

   *Add like terms:* $4\sqrt{5} + 3\sqrt{5} = 7\sqrt{5}$

2) **Simplify** $2\sqrt{7} + 4\sqrt{7} =$

   *Add like terms:* $2\sqrt{7} + 4\sqrt{7} = 6\sqrt{7}$

✎ *Simplify.*

1) $9\sqrt{5} + 4\sqrt{5} =$

2) $4\sqrt{20} - 3\sqrt{20} =$

3) $3\sqrt{22} - 4\sqrt{22} =$

4) $14\sqrt{7} + 12\sqrt{7} =$

5) $4\sqrt{3} - \sqrt{27} =$

6) $\sqrt{12} + 5\sqrt{3} =$

7) $-3\sqrt{15} + 3\sqrt{15} =$

8) $-12\sqrt{8} + 3\sqrt{2} =$

9) $5\sqrt{45} - 3\sqrt{5} =$

10) $-3\sqrt{18} - 2\sqrt{2} =$

11) $16\sqrt{35} + 10\sqrt{35} =$

12) $13\sqrt{19} - 7\sqrt{19} =$

# Domain and Range of Radical Functions

**Step-by-step guide:**

- ✓ To find domain and rage of radical functions, remember that having a negative number under the square root symbol is not possible. (for square roots)
- ✓ To find the domain of the function, find all possible values of the variable inside radical.
- ✓ To find the range, plugin the minimum and maximum values of the variable inside radical.

## *Examples:*

Find the domain and range of the radical function. $y = \sqrt{x - 2}$

For domain: Find non-negative values for radicals: $x \geq 2$

$\sqrt{f(x)} \rightarrow f(x) \geq 0$

Then solve $x - 2 \geq 0 \rightarrow x \geq 2$

domain: $x \geq 2$

for range: the range of an radical function of the form $c\sqrt{ax + b} + k$ is $f(x) \geq k$

$k = 0$ then: $f(x) \geq 0$

✎ *Identify the domain and range of each.*

1) $y = \sqrt{x + 5}$

2) $y = \sqrt{x - 1} - 1$

3) $y = \sqrt{x - 3} + 7$

4) $y = \sqrt{x + 1} - 4$

✎ *Sketch the graph of each function.*

5) $y = \sqrt{x} + 2$

6) $y = 2\sqrt{x} - 5$

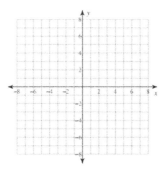

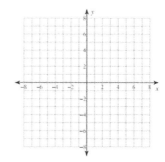

# Radical Equations

**Step-by-step guide:**

- ✓ Isolate the radical on one side of the equation.
- ✓ Square both sides of the equation to remove the radical
- ✓ Solve the equation for the variable
- ✓ Plugin the answer into the original equation to avoid extraneous values.

## *Examples:*

1) Solve $\sqrt{x} - 8 = 12$

   Add 8 to both sides: $\sqrt{x} = 20$

   Square both sides: $(\sqrt{x})^2 = 20^2 \rightarrow x = 400$

2) Solve $\sqrt{x+2} = 6$

   Square both sides: $(\sqrt{(x+2)})^2 = 6^2 \rightarrow x + 2 = 36 \rightarrow x = 34$

✍ *Solve each equation. Remember to check for extraneous solutions.*

1) $\sqrt{x-4} = 2$

2) $6 = \sqrt{x-5}$

3) $\sqrt{x+8} = 12$

4) $\sqrt{x+14} = 10$

5) $9 = \sqrt{x-8}$

6) $21 = \sqrt{x-5}$

7) $12 = \sqrt{x+4}$

8) $2\sqrt{x+8} = 14$

9) $\sqrt{x+5} - 1 = 16$

10) $\sqrt{2x} = \sqrt{3x-8}$

11) $\sqrt{4x+10} = \sqrt{x+12}$

12) $\sqrt{x} = \sqrt{2x-16}$

# Answers – Chapter 8

## Simplifying radical expressions

1) $5x$

2) $30x$

3) $10x$

4) $5\sqrt{5a}$

5) $6\sqrt{6v}$

6) $15x\sqrt{2}$

7) $9\sqrt{5}$

8) $16p\sqrt{2p}$

9) $6m^2\sqrt{6}$

10) $2x.\,y\sqrt{66xy}$

11) $7x\,.\,y\sqrt{xy}$

12) $2a^2\,.\,b\,\sqrt{2b}$

## Simplifying Radical Expressions Involving Fractions

1) $\dfrac{\sqrt{5}}{m}$

2) $\dfrac{8\sqrt{6x}}{x}$

3) $-1$

4) $\dfrac{3\sqrt{6}+4}{2}$

5) $4x^2\sqrt{y}$

6) $6k$

7) $\dfrac{a-\sqrt{ab}}{a-b}$

8) $3-\sqrt{7}$

9) $\dfrac{3-\sqrt{5}+3\sqrt{2}-\sqrt{10}}{4}$

10) $\dfrac{12+2\sqrt{3}+6\sqrt{5}+\sqrt{15}}{33}$

11) $\dfrac{\sqrt{35}-\sqrt{14}+5\sqrt{10}}{3}$

12) $\dfrac{24-3\sqrt{10}-4\sqrt{14}+\sqrt{35}}{27}$

## Multiplying radical expressions

1) $12$

2) $270$

3) $560$

4) $672$

5) $960$

6) $30$

7) $23a\sqrt{a}$

8) $4k^2\sqrt{10k}$

9) $2x^2\sqrt{6x}$

10) $12x^2\sqrt{35}$

11) $84x^2\sqrt{3x}$

12) $108x^3\sqrt{5}$

## Adding and Subtracting Radical Expressions

1) $13\sqrt{5}$

2) $\sqrt{20}$

3) $-\sqrt{22}$

4) $26\sqrt{7}$

7) $0$

8) $-21\sqrt{2}$

9) $12\sqrt{5}$

10) $-11\sqrt{2}$

5) $\sqrt{3}$

11) $26\sqrt{35}$

6) $7\sqrt{3}$

12) $6\sqrt{19}$

## *Domain and Range of Radical Functions*

1) domain: $x \geq -5$

   range: $y \geq 0$

3) domain: $x \geq 3$

   range: $y \geq 7$

2) domain: {all real numbers}

   range: {all real numbers}

4) domain: {all real numbers}

   range: {all real numbers}

5)

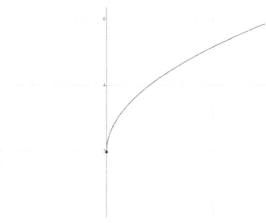

6)

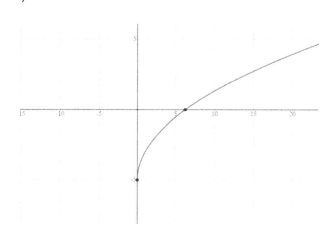

## *Radical Equations*

1) {8}

2) {41}

3) {136}

4) {86}

5) {89}

6) {446}

7) {140}

8) {41}

9) {284}

10) {8}

11) $\{\frac{2}{3}\}$

12) {16}

# Chapter 9:
# Rational Expressions

**Topics that you'll learn in this chapter:**

- ✓ Simplifying Rational Expressions
- ✓ Graphing Rational Expressions
- ✓ Multiplying Rational Expressions
- ✓ Dividing Rational Expressions
- ✓ Adding and Subtracting Rational Expressions
- ✓ Rational Equations
- ✓ Simplify Complex Fractions

*Mathematics is the door and key to the sciences. ~ Roger Bacon*

# Simplifying Rational Expressions

**Step-by-step guide:**

- ✓ Factorize numerator and denominator if they are factorable.
- ✓ Find common factors of both numerator and denominator.
- ✓ Remove the common factor in both numerator and denominator.
- ✓ Simplify if needed.

## Examples:

1) Simplify $\dfrac{9x^2y}{3y^2}$

Cancel the common factor 3: $\dfrac{9x^2y}{3y^2} = \dfrac{3x^2y}{y^2}$

Cancel the common factor $y$: $\dfrac{3x^2y}{y^2} = \dfrac{3x^2}{y}$

Then: $\dfrac{9x^2y}{3y^2} = \dfrac{3x^2}{y}$

2) Simplify $\dfrac{x^2+5x-6}{x+6}$

Factor $x^2 + 5x - 6 = (x-1)(x+6)$

Then: $\dfrac{x^2+5x-6}{x+6} = \dfrac{(x-1)(x+6)}{x+6}$

Cancel the common factor: $(x+6)$

Then: $\dfrac{(x-1)(x+6)}{x+6} = x - 1$

✍ **Simplify.**

1) $\dfrac{16 \quad 3}{20x^3} =$

2) $\dfrac{64 \quad 3}{24x} =$

3) $\dfrac{25 \quad 5}{15x^3} =$

4) $\dfrac{16}{2x-2} =$

5) $\dfrac{15x-3}{24} =$

6) $\dfrac{4x+16}{28} =$

7) $\dfrac{x^2-10x+2}{x-5} =$

8) $\dfrac{x^2-49}{x^2+3x-28} =$

9) $\dfrac{x^2+4x+4}{x^2-5x-14} =$

# Graphing Rational Expressions

**Step-by-step guide:**
- ✓ Find the vertical asymptotes of the function, if there is any. (Vertical asymptotes are vertical lines which correspond to the zeroes of the denominator)
- ✓ Find horizontal or slant asymptote. (If numerator has a bigger degree than denominator, there will be slant asymptote.)
- ✓ If denominator has a bigger degree than numerator, the horizontal asymptote is the x-axes or the line y=0. If they have the same degree, the horizontal asymptote equals the leading coefficient (the coefficient of the largest exponent) of the numerator divided by the leading coefficient of the denominator.
- ✓ Find intercepts and plug in some values of x and solve for y and graph

## *Examples:*

*Graph rational expressions.* $f(x) = \frac{x^2 - x + 2}{x - 1}$

Domain: $\begin{bmatrix} solution: x < 1 \ or \ x > 1 \\ interval \ notation: (-\infty, 1) \cup (1, \infty) \end{bmatrix}$

Range:

$\begin{bmatrix} solution: f(x) \leq -2\sqrt{6} + 3 \ or \ f(x) \geq 2\sqrt{6} + 3 \\ interval \ notation: (-\infty, -2\sqrt{6} + 3] \cup [2\sqrt{6} + 3, \infty) \end{bmatrix}$

Axis interception points of $\frac{x^2 - x + 2}{x - 1}$: $y$ Interceptions: $(0, -2)$

Asymptotes of $\frac{x^2 - x + 2}{x - 1}$: vertical: $x = 1$, horizontal: $y = 2x + 1$

Extreme points of $\frac{x^2 - x + 2}{x - 1}$: Maximum $(\frac{2 - \sqrt{6}}{2}, -\frac{4\sqrt{3} - 3\sqrt{2}}{\sqrt{2}})$, Minimum $(\frac{2 + \sqrt{6}}{2}, \frac{4\sqrt{3} + 3\sqrt{2}}{\sqrt{2}})$

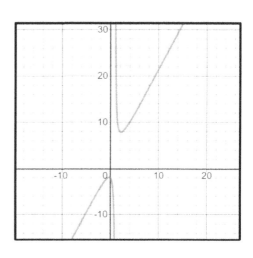

✎ *Graph rational expressions.*

1) $f(x) = \frac{x^2 + 2x - 4}{x - 2}$

2) $f(x) = \frac{4x^3 - 16x + 64}{x^2 - 2x - 4}$

# Multiplying Rational Expressions

**Step-by-step guide:**

✓ Multiplying rational expressions is the same as multiplying fractions. First, multiply numerators and then multiply denominators. Then, simplify as needed.

## *Examples:*

1) **Solve** $\dfrac{x+4}{x-2} \times \dfrac{x-2}{3} =$

Multiply fractions: $\dfrac{x+4}{x-2} \times \dfrac{x-2}{3} = \dfrac{(x+4)(x-2)}{3(x-2)}$

Cancel the common factor: $(x-2)$

then: $\dfrac{(x+4)(x-2)}{3(x-2)} = \dfrac{(x+4)}{3}$

2) **Solve** $\dfrac{x-5}{x+3} \times \dfrac{2x+6}{x-5} =$

Multiply fractions: $\dfrac{x-5}{x+3} \times \dfrac{2x+6}{x-5} = \dfrac{(x-5)(2x+6)}{(x+3)(x-5)}$

Cancel the common factor: $\dfrac{(x-5)(2x+6)}{(x+3)(x-5)} = \dfrac{(2x+6)}{(x+3)}$

Factor $2x+6 = 2(x+3)$

Then: $\dfrac{2(x+3)}{(x+3)} = 2$

✎ *Simplify each expression.*

1) $\dfrac{79x}{25} \cdot \dfrac{85}{27x^2} =$

2) $\dfrac{96}{38} \cdot \dfrac{25}{45} =$

3) $\dfrac{84}{3} \cdot \dfrac{48}{95} =$

4) $\dfrac{53}{43} \cdot \dfrac{46}{31}^{\,2} =$

5) $\dfrac{93}{21} \cdot \dfrac{34}{51x} =$

6) $\dfrac{5x+50}{x+10} \cdot \dfrac{x-2}{5} =$

7) $\dfrac{x-7}{x+6} \cdot \dfrac{10x+60}{x-7} =$

8) $\dfrac{1}{x+10} \cdot \dfrac{10x+30}{x+3} =$

# Dividing Rational Expressions

**Step-by-step guide:**

- ✓ To divide rational expression, use the same method we use for dividing fractions.
- ✓ Keep, Change, Flip
- ✓ Keep first rational expression, change division sign to multiplication, and flip the numerator and denominator of the second rational expression. Then, multiply numerators and multiply denominators. Simplify as needed.

## *Examples:*

1) **Solve** $\dfrac{8x}{5} \div \dfrac{12}{7} =$

$\dfrac{8x}{5} \div \dfrac{12}{7} = \dfrac{\frac{8x}{5}}{\frac{12}{7}}$ , Use Divide fractions rules: $\dfrac{\frac{a}{b}}{\frac{c}{d}} = \dfrac{a \cdot d}{b \cdot c}$

$\dfrac{\frac{8x}{5}}{\frac{12}{7}} = \dfrac{8x \times 7}{12 \times 5} = \dfrac{56x}{60}$

2) **Solve** $\dfrac{2x}{x + 5} \div \dfrac{x}{2x + 10} =$

$\dfrac{\frac{2x}{x+5}}{\frac{x}{2x+10}}$ , Use Divide fractions rules: $\dfrac{(2x)(2x+1\ )}{(x)(x+5)}$

Cancel common fraction: $\dfrac{(2x)(2x+10)}{(x)(x+5)} = \dfrac{2(2x+10)}{(x+5)} = \dfrac{4(x+5)}{(x+5)} = 4$

## ✎ *Divide.*

1) $\dfrac{12x}{3} \div \dfrac{5}{8} =$

5) $\dfrac{5x}{x - 10} \div \dfrac{5x}{x - 5} =$

2) $\dfrac{10x^2}{7} \div \dfrac{3x}{12} =$

6) $\dfrac{x^2 + 10 + 16}{x^2 + 6x + 8} \div \dfrac{1}{x + 8} =$

3) $\dfrac{x + 5}{5x^2 - 10x} \div \dfrac{1}{5x} =$

7) $\dfrac{x^2 - 2x - 15}{8x + 20} \div \dfrac{2}{4x + 10} =$

4) $\dfrac{x - 2}{x + 6x - 12} \div \dfrac{x}{x + 3} =$

8) $\dfrac{x - 4}{x^2 - 2x - 8} \div \dfrac{1}{x - 5} =$

# Adding and Subtracting Rational Expressions

**Step-by-step guide:**

- ✓ For adding and subtracting rational expressions:
- ✓ Find least common denominator (LCD).
- ✓ Write each expression using the LCD.
- ✓ Add or subtract the numerators.
- ✓ Simplify as needed.

## *Examples:*

1) **Solve** $\dfrac{3}{2x+5} + \dfrac{x-2}{2x+5} =$

Use this rule: $\dfrac{a}{c} \pm \dfrac{b}{c} = \dfrac{a \pm b}{c} \rightarrow \dfrac{3}{2x+5} + \dfrac{x-2}{2x+5} = \dfrac{3(x-2)}{2x+5} = \dfrac{3x-6}{2x+5}$

2) **Solve** $\dfrac{x+4}{x-8} + \dfrac{x-4}{x+6} =$

Least common multiplier of $(x-8)$ and $(x+6)$: $(x-8)(x+6)$

Then: $\dfrac{(x+4)(x+6)}{(x-8)(x+6)} + \dfrac{(x-4)(x-8)}{(x+6)(x-8)} = \dfrac{(x+4)(x+6)+(x-4)(x-8)}{(x+6)(x-6)}$

Expand: $(x+4)(x+6) + (x-4)(x-8) = 2x^2 - 2x + 56$

Then: $\dfrac{2x^2-2x+56}{(x+6)(x-8)}$

## ✎ *Simplify each expression*.

1) $\dfrac{2}{6x+10} + \dfrac{x-6}{6x+10} =$

2) $\dfrac{4}{x+1} - \dfrac{2}{x+2} =$

3) $\dfrac{2x}{5x+4} + \dfrac{6x}{2x+3} =$

4) $\dfrac{4x}{x+2} + \dfrac{x-3}{x+1} =$

5) $\dfrac{x}{3x+2} + \dfrac{3x}{2x+3} =$

6) $\dfrac{x+5}{4x^2+20} - \dfrac{x-5}{4x^2+20x} =$

7) $\dfrac{2}{x^2-5x+4} + \dfrac{2}{x^2-4} =$

8) $\dfrac{x-7}{x^2-16} - \dfrac{x-1}{16-x^2} =$

# Rational Equations

**Step-by-step guide:**

- ✓ For solving rational equations, we can use following methods:
- ✓ Converting to a common denominator: In this method, you need to get a common denominator for both sides of equation Then make numerators equal and solve for the variable.
- ✓ Cross-multiplying: This method is useful when there is only one fraction on each side of the equation. Simply multiply first numerator by second denominator and make the result equal to the product of second numerator and first denominator.

***Examples:*** Solve $\dfrac{x-2}{x+1} = \dfrac{x+5}{x-2}$

Use fraction cross multiply: if $\dfrac{a}{b} = \dfrac{c}{d}$ then: $a.\, d = b.\, c$
Then: $(x-2)(x-2) = (x+5)(x+1)$
Simplify: $(x-2)^2 = (x+5)(x+1)$
Expand: $(x-2)^2 = x^2 - 4x + 4$
Expand: $(x+5)(x+1) = x^2 + 6x + 5$
Then: $x^2 - 4x + 4 = x^2 + 6x + 5$
Simplify: $x^2 - 4x = x^2 + 6x + 1$
Subtract both sides: $x^2 + 6x$
Then: $-10x = 1 \rightarrow x = -\dfrac{1}{10}$

✍ *Solve each equation. Remember to check for extraneous solutions.*

1) $\dfrac{2x-3}{x+1} = \dfrac{x+6}{x-2}$

2) $\dfrac{3x-2}{9x+1} = \dfrac{2x-5}{6x-5}$

3) $\dfrac{1}{n-8} - 1 = \dfrac{7}{n-8}$

4) $\dfrac{x+5}{x^2-2x} - 1 = \dfrac{1}{x^2-2x}$

5) $\dfrac{x-2}{x+3} - 1 = \dfrac{1}{x+2}$

6) $\dfrac{1}{6x^2} = \dfrac{1}{3x^2} - \dfrac{1}{x}$

7) $\dfrac{x+5}{x^2-x} = \dfrac{1}{x^2+x} - \dfrac{x-6}{x+1}$

8) $1 = \dfrac{1}{x^2-2x} + \dfrac{x-1}{x}$

# Simplify Complex Fractions

- ✓ Convert mixed numbers to improper fractions.
- ✓ Simplify all fractions.
- ✓ Write the fraction in the numerator of the main fraction line then write division sing (÷) and the fraction of the denominator.
- ✓ Use normal method for dividing fractions.
- ✓ Simplify as needed.

*Examples:* Solve $\dfrac{\frac{2}{5}}{\frac{2}{25} - \frac{5}{16}}$

Use the fraction rule: $\dfrac{\frac{b}{c}}{a} = \dfrac{b}{c \cdot a}$

$$\dfrac{\frac{2}{5}}{\frac{2}{25} - \frac{5}{16}} = \dfrac{2}{5\left(\frac{2}{25} - \frac{5}{16}\right)} = \dfrac{2}{5\left(-\frac{93}{400}\right)} = \dfrac{2}{-5 \cdot \frac{93}{400}} = -\dfrac{2}{5 \cdot \frac{93}{400}} = -\dfrac{2}{\frac{93}{80}}$$

Use the fraction rule: $\dfrac{a}{\frac{b}{c}} = \dfrac{a \cdot c}{b} \rightarrow -\dfrac{2}{\frac{93}{80}} = -\dfrac{2 \cdot 80}{93} = -\dfrac{160}{93}$

## ✎ *Simplify each expression.*

1) $\dfrac{\frac{12}{3}}{\frac{2}{15}} =$

2) $\dfrac{8}{\frac{8}{x} + \frac{2}{3x}} =$

3) $\dfrac{x}{\frac{2}{5} - \frac{2}{x}} =$

4) $\dfrac{\frac{2}{x+2}}{\frac{8}{x^2 + 6x + 8}} =$

5) $\dfrac{\frac{12}{x-1}}{\frac{12}{5} - \frac{12}{25}} =$

6) $\dfrac{1 + \frac{2}{x-4}}{1 - \frac{6}{x-4}} =$

7) $\dfrac{\frac{x+6}{4}}{\frac{x^2}{2} - \frac{5}{2}} =$

8) $\dfrac{\frac{x-2}{x-6}}{\frac{8}{x-2} + \frac{2}{9}} =$

# Answers – Chapter 9

## *Simplifying rational expressions*

1) $\frac{4}{5}$

2) $\frac{8x^2}{3}$

3) $\frac{5x^2}{3}$

4) $\frac{8}{x-1}$

5) $\frac{5x-1}{8}$

6) $\frac{x+4}{7}$

7) $x-5$

8) $\frac{x-7}{x-4}$

9) $\frac{x+2}{x-7}$

## *Graphing rational expressions*

1)

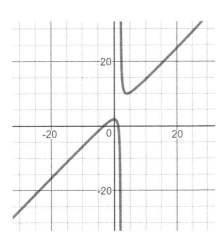

2)

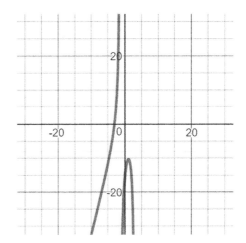

## *Multiplying rational expressions*

1) $\frac{1343}{135x}$

2) $\frac{80}{57x}$

3) $\frac{1344}{95}$

4) $\frac{243^{\ 2}}{1333}$

5) $\frac{62}{21x}$

6) $x-2$

7) $10$

8) $\frac{10}{x+10}$

## *Dividing rational expressions*

9) $6x^2$

10) $\frac{40x}{7}$

11) $\frac{x+5}{x-2}$

12) $\frac{(x-2)(x+3)}{x(7x-12)}$

13) $\frac{x^2}{(x-10)(x-5)}$

14) $x+8$

15) $\frac{(x+3)(x-5)}{4}$

16) $\frac{x-5}{x+2}$

## *Adding and subtracting rational expressions*

1) $\dfrac{-4+x}{6x+10}$

2) $\dfrac{2x+6}{(x+1)(x+2)}$

3) $\dfrac{34x^2+30x}{(5x+4)(2x+3)}$

4) $\dfrac{5x^2+3x-6}{(x+2)(x+1)}$

5) $\dfrac{11^2+9x}{(3x+2)(2x+3)}$

6) $\dfrac{5}{2x(x+5)}$

7) $\dfrac{4x^2-10x}{(x-1)(x-4)(x+2)(x-2)}$

8) $\dfrac{2}{x+4}$

## Solving Rational Equations

1) $\{0, 14\}$

2) $\{\frac{1}{6}\}$

3) $\{2\}$

4) $\{4, -1\}$

5) $\{-\frac{19}{8}\}$

6) $\{\frac{1}{6}\}$

7) $\{-\frac{1}{4}\}$

8) $\{4, 1\}$

## Simplify complex fractions

1) $30$

2) $\dfrac{12x}{13}$

3) $\dfrac{5x^2}{2x-10}$

4) $\dfrac{(x+4)}{4}$

5) $\dfrac{25}{4x-4}$

6) $\dfrac{x-2}{x-10}$

7) $\dfrac{x+6}{2x^2-10}$

8) $\dfrac{9(x-2)^2}{(2x+68(x-6)}$

9)

# Chapter 10:
# Sequences and Series

**Math Topics that you'll learn in this chapter:**

- ✓ Arithmetic Sequences
- ✓ Geometric Sequences
- ✓ Finite Geometric Series
- ✓ Infinite Geometric Series

*Mathematics is like checkers in being suitable for the young, not too difficult, amusing, and without peril to the state. –*

*Plato*

# Arithmetic Sequences

## Step-by-step guide:

✓ A sequence of numbers such that the difference between the consecutive terms is constant is called arithmetic sequence. For example, the sequence $6, 8, 10, 12, 14, \dots$ is an arithmetic sequence with common difference of 2.

✓ To find any term in an arithmetic sequence use this formula: $x_n = a + d(n - 1)$
$a$ = the first term,     $d$ = the common difference between terms, $n$ = number of items

## Examples:

**1) Find the first three terms of the sequence.** $a_{17} = 38, d = 3$

First, we need to find $a_1$ *or* $a$. Use arithmetic sequence formula: $x_n = a + d(n - 1)$

If $a_8 = 38$, then $n = 8$. Rewrite the formula and put the values provided:

$x_n = a + d(n - 1) \rightarrow 38 = a + 3(3 - 1) = a + 6$, now solve for $a$.

$38 = a + 6 \rightarrow a = 38 - 6 = 32$,

First Five Terms: $32, 35, 38$

**2) Given the first term and the common difference of an arithmetic sequence find the first five terms.** $a_1 = 18, d = 2$

Use arithmetic sequence formula: $x_n = a + d(n - 1)$,

If $n = 1$ then: $x_1 = 18 + 2(1) \rightarrow x_1 = 18$

First Five Terms: $18, 20, 22, 24, 26$

✎ *Find the next three terms of each arithmetic sequence.*

1) $15, 11, 7, 3, -1, \dots$

2) $-21, -14, -7, 0, \dots$

3) $3, 6, 9, 12, 15, \dots$

4) $4, 8, 12, 16, 20, \dots$

✎ *Given the first term and the common difference of an arithmetic sequence find the first five terms and the explicit formula.*

5) $a_1 = 24, d = 2$

6) $a_1 = -15, d = -5$

7) $a_1 = 18, d = 10$

8) $a_1 = -38, d = -10$

# Geometric Sequences

## Step-by-step guide:

✓ It is a sequence of numbers where each term after the first is found by multiplying the previous item by the common ratio, a fixed, non-zero number. For example, the sequence 2, 4, 8, 16, 32, … is a geometric sequence with common ratio of 2.

✓ To find any term in a geometric sequence use this formula: $x_n = ar^{(n-1)}$

$a$ = the first term,       $r$ = the common ratio, $n$ = number of items

## Examples:

1) **Given the first term and the common ratio of a geometric sequence find the first five terms of the sequence.** $a_1 = 3, r = -2$

   Use geometric sequence formula: $x_n = ar^{(n-1)} \rightarrow x_n = 0.8 \cdot (-5)^{n-1}$

   If $n = 1$ then: $x_1 = 3 \cdot (-2)^{1-1} = 3\,(1) = 3$, First Five Terms: $3, -6, 12, -24, 48$

2) **Given two terms in a geometric sequence find the 8th term.** $a_3 = 10$ **and** $a_5 = 40$

   Use geometric sequence formula: $x_n = ar^{(n-1)} \rightarrow a_3 = ar^{(3-1)} = ar^2 = 10$

   $$x_n = ar^{(n-1)} \rightarrow a_5 = ar^{(5-1)} = ar^4 = 40$$

   Now divide $a_5$ by $a_3$. Then: $\frac{a_5}{a_3} = \frac{ar^4}{ar^2} = \frac{40}{10}$, Now simplify: $\frac{ar^4}{ar^2} = \frac{40}{10} \rightarrow r^2 = 4 \rightarrow r = 2$

   We can find $a$ now: $ar^2 = 12 \rightarrow a(2^2) = 10 \rightarrow a = 2.5$

   Use the formula to find the $8^{th}$ term: $x_n = ar^{(n-1)} \rightarrow a_8 = (2.5)(2)^8 = 2.5(256) = 640$

✎ **Determine if the sequence is geometric. If it is, find the common ratio.**

1) $1, -5, 25, -125, …$          3) $4, 16, 36, 64, …$
2) $-2, -4, -8, -16, …$          4) $-3, -15, -75, -375, …$

✎ **Given the first term and the common ratio of a geometric sequence find the first five terms and the explicit formula.**

5) $a_1 = 0.8, r = -5$
6) $a_1 = 1, r = 2$

# Finite Geometric Series

**Step-by-step guide:**

✓ The sum of a geometric series is finite when the absolute value of the ratio is less than 1.
✓ Finite Geometric Series formula: $S_n = \sum_{i=1}^{n} ar^{i-1} = a_1\left(\frac{1-r^n}{1-r}\right)$

*Examples:*

*Evaluate each geometric series described.*

**1)** $\sum_{n=1}^{5} 3^{n-1}$

Use this formula: $S_n = \sum_{i=1}^{n} ar^{i-1} = a_1\left(\frac{1-r^n}{1-r}\right) \rightarrow \sum_{n=1}^{5} 3^{n-1} = (1)\left(\frac{1-3^5}{1-3}\right)$

$\rightarrow (1)\left(\frac{1-3^5}{1-3}\right) = 121$

**2)** $\sum_{n=1}^{3} -4^{n-1}$

Use this formula: $S_n = \sum_{i=1}^{n} ar^{i-1} = a_1\left(\frac{1-r^n}{1-r}\right) \rightarrow \sum_{n=1}^{3} -4^{n-1} = (-1)\left(\frac{1-4^3}{1-4}\right)$

$\rightarrow (-1)\left(\frac{1-4^3}{1-4}\right) = -21$

✍ *Evaluate each geometric series described.*

1) $1 + 2 + 4 + 8 \ldots, n = 6$          _____

2) $1 - 4 + 16 - 64 \ldots, n = 9$          _____

3) $-2 - 6 - 18 - 54 \ldots, n = 9$          _____

4) $2 - 10 + 50 - 250 \ldots, n = 8$          _____

5) $1 - 5 + 25 - 125 \ldots, n = 7$          _____

6) $-3 - 6 - 12 - 24 \ldots, n = 9$          _____

# Infinite Geometric Series

**Step-by-step guide:**

✓ Infinite Geometric Series: The sum of a geometric series is infinite when the absolute value of the ratio is more than 1.

✓ Infinite Geometric Series formula: $S = \sum_{i=0}^{\infty} a_i r^i = \frac{a_1}{1-r}$

## Examples:

1) **Evaluate infinite geometric series described.** $\sum_{i=1}^{\infty} 9^{i-1}$

Use this formula: $\sum_{i=0}^{\infty} a_i r^i = \frac{a_1}{1-r} \rightarrow \sum_{i=1}^{\infty} 9^{i-1} = \frac{1}{1-9} = \frac{1}{-8} = -\frac{1}{8}$

2) **Evaluate infinite geometric series described.** $\sum_{k=1}^{\infty} (\frac{1}{4})^{k-1}$

Use this formula: $\sum_{i=0}^{\infty} a_i r^i = \frac{a_1}{1-r} \rightarrow \sum_{k=1}^{\infty} (\frac{1}{4})^{k-1} = \frac{1}{1-\frac{1}{4}} = \frac{1}{\frac{3}{4}} = \frac{4}{3}$

✎ **Determine if each geometric series converges or diverges.**

1) $a_1 = -1, r = 3$

2) $a_1 = 3.2, r = 0.2$

3) $a_1 = 5, r = 2$

4) $-1, 3, -9, 27, \ldots$

5) $2, -1, \frac{1}{2}, -\frac{1}{4}, \frac{1}{8}, \ldots$

6) $81 + 27 + 9 + 3 \ldots$

✎ **Evaluate each infinite geometric series described.**

7) $\sum_{k=1}^{\infty} 4^{k-1}$

8) $\sum_{i=1}^{\infty} 5 \cdot (-\frac{1}{5})^{i-1}$

9) $\sum_{k=1}^{\infty} (-\frac{1}{3})^{k-1}$

10) $\sum_{n=1}^{\infty} 16(\frac{1}{4})^{n-1}$

84

# Answers – Chapter 10

## Arithmetic Sequences

1) $-5, -9, -13$
2) $7, 14, 21$
3) $18, 21, 24$
4) $24, 28, 32$
5) First Five Terms: $24, 26, 28, 30, 32$, Explicit: $a_n = 2n + 22$
6) First Five Terms: $-15, -20, -25, -30, -35$, Explicit: $a_n = -5n - 10$
7) First Five Terms: $18, 28, 38, 48, 58$, Explicit: $a_n = 10n + 8$
8) First Five Terms: $-38, -138, -238, -338, -438$, Explicit: $a_n = -100n + 62$

## Geometric Sequences

1) $r = -5$
2) $r = 2$
3) not geometric
4) $r = 5$
5) First Five Terms: $0.8, -4, 20, -100, 500$

   Explicit: $a_n = 0.8 \cdot (-5)^{n-1}$

6) First Five Terms: $1, 2, 4, 8, 16$

   Explicit: $a_n = 2^{n-1}$

## Finite Geometric

1) $63$
2) $52,429$
3) $-19,682$
4) $-130,208$
5) $13,021$
6) $-513$

## Infinite Geometric

1) Diverges
2) Converges
3) Converges
4) Diverges
5) Converges
6) Converges
7) Infinite
8) $\frac{25}{6}$
9) $\frac{3}{4}$
10) $\frac{64}{3}$

# CLEP College Algebra Test Review

College-Level Examination Program (CLEP) is a series of 33 standardized tests that measures your knowledge of certain subjects. You can earn college credit at thousands of colleges and universities by earning a satisfactory score on a computer-based CLEP exam.

The CLEP College Algebra measures your knowledge of math topics generally taught in a one-semester college course in algebra. It contains approximately 60 multiple choice questions to be answered in 90 minutes. Some of these questions are pretest questions that will not be scored. These 60 questions cover: basic algebraic operations; linear and quadratic equations, inequalities, and graphs; algebraic, exponential, and logarithmic functions; and miscellaneous other topics. A scientific calculator is available to students during the entire testing time.

The CLEP College Algebra exam score ranges from 20 to 80 converting to A, B, C, or D based on this score. The letter grade is applied to your college course equivalent.

In this section, there are two complete CLEP College Algebra Tests. Take these tests to see what score you'll be able to receive on a real CLEP College Algebra test.

Good luck!

# Time to Test

## Time to refine your quantitative reasoning skill with a practice test

Take a CLEP College Algebra test to simulate the test day experience. After you've finished, score your test using the answer keys.

## Before You Start

- You'll need a pencil, a calculator and a timer to take the test.

- For most multiple questions, there are five possible answers. Choose which one is best.

- It's okay to guess. There is no penalty for wrong answers.

- Use the answer sheet provided to record your answers.

- **Calculator is permitted for CLEP College Algebra Test.**

- After you've finished the test, review the answer key to see where you went wrong.

**Good Luck!**

# CLEP College Algebra
# Practice Test 1

# 2020

**Total number of questions:** 60

**Total time:** 90 Minutes

**Calculator is permitted for CLEP College Algebra Test.**

# CLEP College Algebra Practice Test Answer Sheet

Remove (or photocopy) this answer sheet and use it to complete the practice test.

| CLEP College Algebra Practice Test 1 Answer Sheet | | |
|---|---|---|
| 1 (A) (B) (C) (D) (E) | 21 (A) (B) (C) (D) (E) | 41 (A) (B) (C) (D) (E) |
| 2 (A) (B) (C) (D) (E) | 22 (A) (B) (C) (D) (E) | 42 (A) (B) (C) (D) (E) |
| 3 (A) (B) (C) (D) (E) | 23 (A) (B) (C) (D) (E) | 43 (A) (B) (C) (D) (E) |
| 4 (A) (B) (C) (D) (E) | 24 (A) (B) (C) (D) (E) | 44 (A) (B) (C) (D) (E) |
| 5 (A) (B) (C) (D) (E) | 25 (A) (B) (C) (D) (E) | 45 (A) (B) (C) (D) (E) |
| 6 (A) (B) (C) (D) (E) | 26 (A) (B) (C) (D) (E) | 46 (A) (B) (C) (D) (E) |
| 7 (A) (B) (C) (D) (E) | 27 (A) (B) (C) (D) (E) | 47 (A) (B) (C) (D) (E) |
| 8 (A) (B) (C) (D) (E) | 28 (A) (B) (C) (D) (E) | 48 (A) (B) (C) (D) (E) |
| 9 (A) (B) (C) (D) (E) | 29 (A) (B) (C) (D) (E) | 49 (A) (B) (C) (D) (E) |
| 10 (A) (B) (C) (D) (E) | 30 (A) (B) (C) (D) (E) | 50 (A) (B) (C) (D) (E) |
| 11 (A) (B) (C) (D) (E) | 31 (A) (B) (C) (D) (E) | 51 (A) (B) (C) (D) (E) |
| 12 (A) (B) (C) (D) (E) | 32 (A) (B) (C) (D) (E) | 52 (A) (B) (C) (D) (E) |
| 13 (A) (B) (C) (D) (E) | 33 (A) (B) (C) (D) (E) | 53 (A) (B) (C) (D) (E) |
| 14 (A) (B) (C) (D) (E) | 34 (A) (B) (C) (D) (E) | 54 (A) (B) (C) (D) (E) |
| 15 (A) (B) (C) (D) (E) | 35 (A) (B) (C) (D) (E) | 55 (A) (B) (C) (D) (E) |
| 16 (A) (B) (C) (D) (E) | 36 (A) (B) (C) (D) (E) | 56 (A) (B) (C) (D) (E) |
| 17 (A) (D) (C) (D) (E) | 37 (A) (B) (C) (D) (E) | 57 (A) (B) (C) (D) (E) |
| 18 (A) (B) (C) (D) (E) | 38 (A) (B) (C) (D) (E) | 58 (A) (B) (C) (D) (E) |
| 19 (A) (B) (C) (D) (E) | 39 (A) (B) (C) (D) (E) | 59 (A) (B) (C) (D) (E) |
| 20 (A) (B) (C) (D) (E) | 40 (A) (B) (C) (D) (E) | 60 (A) (B) (C) (D) (E) |

1) If $f(x) = 2x + 2$ and $g(x) = x^2 + 4x$, then find $(\frac{f}{g})(x)$.

A. $\dfrac{2x+2}{x^2+4x}$

B. $\dfrac{x+1}{x^2+2x}$

C. $\dfrac{2x+2}{x^2+1}$

D. $\dfrac{2x+2}{x^2+x}$

E. $\dfrac{x^2+4x}{2x+2}$

2) In the standard $(x, y)$ coordinate plane, which of the following lines contains the points $(3, -5)$ and $(8, 15)$?

A. $y = 4x - 17$

B. $y = \dfrac{1}{4}x + 13$

C. $y = -4x + 7$

D. $y = -\dfrac{1}{4}x + 17$

E. $y = 2x - 11$

3) Which of the following is equal to the expression below?
$$(5x + 2y)(2x - y)$$

A. $4x^2 - 2y^2$

B. $2x^2 + 6xy - 2y^2$

C. $24x^2 + 2xy - 2y^2$

D. $10x^2 - xy - 2y^2$

E. $8x^2 + 2xy - 2y^2$

4) What is the product of all possible values of $x$ in the following equation? $|x - 10| = 4$

A. 3

B. 7

C. 13

D. 84

E. 100

5) What is the slope of a line that is perpendicular to the line $4x - 2y = 6$?

A. $-2$

B. $-\dfrac{1}{2}$

C. 4

D. 12

E. 14

6) What is the value of the expression $6(x - 2y) + (2 - x)^2$ when $x = 3$ and $= -2$ ?
   A. $-4$
   B. $20$
   C. $43$
   D. $50$
   E. $80$

7) For $i = \sqrt{-1}$, which of the following is equivalent of $\frac{2+3i}{5-2i}$ ?
   A. $\frac{3+2i}{5}$
   B. $5+3i$
   C. $\frac{4+19}{29}$
   D. $\frac{4+19i}{20}$
   E. $\frac{4+21i}{20}$

8) If function is defined as $f(x) = bx^2 + 15$, and $b$ is a constant and $f(2) = 35$. What is the value of $f(3)$?
   A. $25$
   B. $35$
   C. $60$
   D. $65$
   E. $75$

9) What is the area of a square whose diagonal is 4?
   A. $4$
   B. $8$
   C. $16$
   D. $64$
   E. $124$

10) The average of five numbers is 26. If a sixth number 42 is added, then, what is the new average? (round your answer to the nearest hundredth)
   A. $25$
   B. $26.5$
   C. $27$
   D. $28.66$
   E. $36$

11) A construction company is building a wall. The company can build 30 cm of the wall per minute. After 40 minutes $\frac{3}{4}$ of the wall is completed. How many meters is the wall?

   A. 6

   B. 8

   C. 14

   D. 16

   E. 20

12) What is the solution of the following inequality?

$$|x - 2| \geq 3$$

   A. $x \geq 5 \cup x \leq -1$

   B. $-1 \leq x \leq 5$

   C. $x \geq 5$

   D. $x \leq -1$

   E. Set of real numbers

13) When 5 times the number $x$ is added to 10, the result is 35. What is the result when 3 times $x$ is added to 6?

   A. 10

   B. 15

   C. 21

   D. 25

   E. 28

14) If $3h + g = 8h + 4$, what is $g$ in terms of $h$?

   A. $h = 5g - 4$

   B. $g = 5h + 4$

   C. $h = 4g$

   D. $g = h + 1$

   E. $g = 5h + 1$

15) What is the value of $x$ in the following equation? $\frac{2}{3}x + \frac{1}{6} = \frac{1}{2}$

   A. 6

   B. $\frac{1}{2}$

   C. $\frac{1}{3}$

   D. $\frac{1}{4}$

   E. $\frac{1}{12}$

16) A bank is offering 4.5% simple interest on a savings account. If you deposit $12,000, how much interest will you earn in two years?
   A. $420
   B. $1,080
   C. $4,200
   D. $8,400
   E. $9,600

17) Simplify $7x^2y^3(2x^2y)^3 =$

   A. $12x^4y^6$
   B. $12x^8y^6$
   C. $56x^4y^6$
   D. $56x^8y^6$
   E. $96x^8y^6$

18) What are the zeroes of the function $f(x) = x^3 + 7x^2 + 12x$?
   A. $0$
   B. $-4, -3$
   C. $0, 2, 3$
   D. $-3, -5$
   E. $0, -3, -4$

19) If $x + sin^2a + cos^2a = 3$, then $x$ = ?
   A. $1$
   B. $2$
   C. $3$
   D. $4$
   E. $5$

20) If $\sqrt{3x} = \sqrt{y}$, then $x =$
   A. $3y$
   B. $\sqrt{\dfrac{y}{3}}$
   C. $\sqrt{3y}$
   D. $y^2$
   E. $\dfrac{y}{3}$

21) If $f(x)=2x^3+5x^2+2x$ and $g(x)=-4$, what is the value of $f(g(x))$?

   A. 56
   B. 32
   C. 24
   D. $-4$
   E. $-56$

22) A cruise line ship left Port A and traveled 50 miles due west and then 120 miles due north. At this point, what is the shortest distance from the cruise to port A?

   A. 70 $miles$
   B. 80 $miles$
   C. 150 $miles$
   D. 230 $miles$
   E. 130 $miles$

23) What is the equivalent temperature of $104°F$ in Celsius?

   $$C = \frac{5}{9}(F-32)$$

   A. 32
   B. 40
   C. 48
   D. 52
   E. 64

24) The perimeter of a rectangular yard is 72 meters. What is its length if its width is twice its length?

   A. 12 $meters$
   B. 18 $meters$
   C. 20 $meters$
   D. 24 $meters$
   E. 36 $meters$

25) The average of 6 numbers is 14. The average of 4 of those numbers is 10. What is the average of the other two numbers?

   A. 10
   B. 12
   C. 14
   D. 22
   E. 24

26) If 150% of a number is 75, then what is the 80% of that number?

   A. 40
   B. 50
   C. 70
   D. 85
   E. 90

27) What is the slope of the line: $4x - 2y = 12$
  A. $-1$
  B. $-2$
  C. $1$
  D. $1.5$
  E. $2$

28) In two successive years, the population of a town is increased by 10% and 20%. What percent of the population is increased after two years?
  A. 30%
  B. 32%
  C. 35%
  D. 68%
  E. 70%

29) The area of a circle is $36\pi$. What is the diameter of the circle?
  A. 4
  B. 8
  C. 12
  D. 14
  E. 16

30) If 20% of a number is 4, what is the number?
  A. 4
  B. 8
  C. 10
  D. 20
  E. 25

31) What is the value of $x$ in the following system of equations?
$$5x + 2y = 3$$
$$y = x$$

  A. $x = \dfrac{3}{7}$

  B. $x = \dfrac{1}{3}$

  C. $x = \dfrac{2}{3}$

  D. $x = \dfrac{4}{3}$

  E. $x = \dfrac{5}{3}$

32) In a hotel, there are 5 floors and $x$ rooms on each floor. If each room has exactly $y$ chairs, which of the following gives the total number of chairs in the hotel?
A. $5xy$
B. $2xy$
C. $x + y$
D. $x + 5y$
E. $2x + 5y$

33) If $\alpha = 2\beta$ and $\beta = 3\gamma$, how many $\alpha$ are equal to $36\gamma$?
A. 12
B. 2
C. 6
D. 4
E. 1

34) If $f(x) = 2x^3 + 5x^2 + 2x$ and $g(x) = -3$, what is the value of $f(g(x))$?
A. 36
B. 32
C. 24
D. 15
E. $-15$

35) The diagonal of a rectangle is 10 inches long and the height of the rectangle is 6 inches. What is the perimeter of the rectangle?
A. $10\ inches$
B. $12\ inches$
C. $16\ inches$
D. $18\ inches$
E. $28\ inches$

36) The perimeter of the trapezoid below is $40\ cm$. What is its area?

A. $48\ cm^2$
B. $98\ cm^2$
C. $140\ cm^2$
D. $576\ cm^2$
E. $986\ cm^2$

37) If $f(x)=2x^3+2$ and $(x)=\frac{1}{x}$, what is the value of $f(g(x))$?

A. $\dfrac{1}{2x^3+2}$

B. $\dfrac{2}{x^3}$

C. $\dfrac{1}{2x}$

D. $\dfrac{1}{2x+2}$

E. $\dfrac{2}{x^3}+2$

38) A cruise line ship left Port $A$ and traveled 80 miles due west and then 150 miles due north.

At this point, what is the shortest distance from the cruise to port $A$?

A. 70 miles

B. 80 miles

C. 150 miles

D. 170 miles

E. 230 miles

39) If the ratio of $5a$ to $2b$ is $\frac{1}{10}$, what is the ratio of $a$ to $b$?

A. 10

B. 25

C. $\dfrac{1}{25}$

D. $\dfrac{1}{20}$

E. $\dfrac{1}{10}$

40) If $x=9$, what is the value of $y$ in the following equation? $2y=\dfrac{2x^2}{3}+6$

A. 30

B. 45

C. 60

D. 120

E. 180

41) If $\frac{x-3}{5} = N$ and $N = 6$, what is the value of $x$?
A. 25
B. 28
C. 30
D. 33
E. 36

42) Which of the following is equal to $b^{\frac{3}{5}}$?
A. $\sqrt{b^{\frac{5}{3}}}$
B. $b^{\frac{5}{3}}$
C. $\sqrt[5]{b^3}$
D. $\sqrt[3]{b^5}$
E. $\sqrt[3]{b^{-5}}$

43) On Saturday, Sara read $N$ pages of a book each hour for 3 hours, and Mary read $M$ pages of a book each hour for 4 hours. Which of the following represents the total number of pages of book read by Sara and Mary on Saturday?
A. $12MN$
B. $3N + 4M$
C. $7MN$
D. $4N + 3M$
E. $4N - 3M$

44) Simplify $(-4 + 9i)(3 + 5i)$.

A. $54 - 7i$
B. $-54 + 7i$
C. $-57 + 7i$
D. $57 - 7i$
E. $-57 - 7i$

45) If function is defined as $f(x) = bx^2 + 15$, and $b$ is a constant and $f(2) = 35$. What is the value of $f(5)$?
A. 25
B. 35
C. 140
D. 165
E. 168

46) Find the solution $(x, y)$ to the following system of equations?
$$2x + 5y = 11$$
$$4x - 2y = -14$$

    A. $(14, 5)$
    B. $(6, 8)$
    C. $(11, 17)$
    D. $(-2, 3)$
    E. $(2, 3)$

47) Calculate $f(4)$ for the function $f(x) = 3x^2 - 4$.
    A. 44
    B. 40
    C. 38
    D. 30
    E. 20

48) What are the zeroes of the function $f(x) = x^3 + 5x^2 + 6x$?

    A. 0
    B. 2
    C. $0, 2, 3$
    D. $0, -2, -3$
    E. $0, -2, 3$

49) Simplify $\frac{4-3i}{-4i}$?
    A. $i$
    B. $\frac{3i}{4}$
    C. $\frac{3}{4} - i$
    D. $\frac{3}{4} + i$
    E. $4 + i$

$$y = x^2 - 7x + 12$$

50) The equation above represents a parabola in the $xy$-plane. Which of the following equivalent forms of the equation displays the $x$-intercepts of the parabola as constants or coefficients?

    A. $y = x + 3$

    B. $y = x(x - 7)$

    C. $y = (x + 3)(x + 4)$

    D. $y = (x - 3)(x - 4)$

    E. $y = (x - 4)(x - 7)$

51) The function $g(x)$ is defined by a polynomial. Some values of $x$ and $g(x)$ are shown in the table below. Which of the following must be a factor of $g(x)$?

| $x$ | $g(x)$ |
|-----|--------|
| 0   | 5      |
| 1   | 4      |
| 2   | 0      |

- A.  $x$
- B.  $x - 1$
- C.  $x - 2$
- D.  $x + 1$
- E.  $x + 6$

52) What is the value of $\frac{4b}{c}$ when $\frac{c}{b} = 2$

- A.  8
- B.  4
- C.  2
- D.  1
- E.  0

53) If $x + 5 = 8, 2y - 1 = 5$ then $xy + 15 =$

- A.  30
- B.  24
- C.  21
- D.  17
- E.  15

54) If $\frac{a-b}{b} = \frac{10}{13}$, then which of the following must be true?

- A.  $\frac{a}{b} = \frac{10}{13}$
- B.  $\frac{a}{b} = \frac{23}{13}$
- C.  $\frac{a}{b} = \frac{13}{21}$
- D.  $\frac{a}{b} = \frac{21}{10}$
- E.  $\frac{a}{b} = \frac{10}{23}$

55) Which of the following lines is parallel to: $6y - 2x = 24$?

- A.  $y = \frac{1}{3}x + 2$
- B.  $y = 3x + 5$
- C.  $y = x - 2$
- D.  $y = 2x - 1$
- E.  $y = -x - 1$

56) The average of $13, 15, 20$ and $x$ is $20$. What is the value of $x$

    A.  9

    B.  15

    C.  18

    D.  32

    E.  36

57) Solve the following equation for $y$?

$$\frac{x}{3+4} = \frac{y}{11-8}$$

    A.  $\frac{3}{5}x$

    B.  $\frac{3}{7}x$

    C.  $3x$

    D.  $x$

    E.  $-x$

58) If the interior angles of a quadrilateral are in the ratio $1:2:3:4$, what is the measure of the smallest angle?

    A.  $36°$

    B.  $72°$

    C.  $108°$

    D.  $144°$

    E.  $154°$

59) Sara orders a box of pen for \$3 per box. A tax of $8.5\%$ is added to the cost of the pens before a flat shipping fee of \$6 closest out the transaction. Which of the following represents total cost of $p$ boxes of pens in dollars?

    A.  $1.085(3p) + 6$

    B.  $6p + 3$

    C.  $1.085(6p) + 3$

    D.  $3p + 6$

    E.  $6p + 6$

60) A plant grows at a linear rate. After five weeks, the plant is $40\ cm$ tall. Which of the following functions represents the relationship between the height $(y)$ of the plant and number of weeks of growth $(x)$?

    A.  $y(x) = 40x + 8$

    B.  $y(x) = 8x + 40$

    C.  $y(x) = 40x$

    D.  $y(x) = 8x$

    E.  $y(x) = 4x$

## End of CLEP College Algebra Practice Test 1

# CLEP College Algebra
# Practice Test 2

# 2020

**Total number of questions:** 60

**Total time:** 90 Minutes

**Calculator is permitted for CLEP College Algebra Test.**

# CLEP College Algebra Practice Test Answer Sheet

Remove (or photocopy) this answer sheet and use it to complete the practice test.

| CLEP College Algebra Practice Test 2 Answer Sheet | | |
|---|---|---|
| 1 Ⓐ Ⓑ Ⓒ Ⓓ Ⓔ | 21 Ⓐ Ⓑ Ⓒ Ⓓ Ⓔ | 41 Ⓐ Ⓑ Ⓒ Ⓓ Ⓔ |
| 2 Ⓐ Ⓑ Ⓒ Ⓓ Ⓔ | 22 Ⓐ Ⓑ Ⓒ Ⓓ Ⓔ | 42 Ⓐ Ⓑ Ⓒ Ⓓ Ⓔ |
| 3 Ⓐ Ⓑ Ⓒ Ⓓ Ⓔ | 23 Ⓐ Ⓑ Ⓒ Ⓓ Ⓔ | 43 Ⓐ Ⓑ Ⓒ Ⓓ Ⓔ |
| 4 Ⓐ Ⓑ Ⓒ Ⓓ Ⓔ | 24 Ⓐ Ⓑ Ⓒ Ⓓ Ⓔ | 44 Ⓐ Ⓑ Ⓒ Ⓓ Ⓔ |
| 5 Ⓐ Ⓑ Ⓒ Ⓓ Ⓔ | 25 Ⓐ Ⓑ Ⓒ Ⓓ Ⓔ | 45 Ⓐ Ⓑ Ⓒ Ⓓ Ⓔ |
| 6 Ⓐ Ⓑ Ⓒ Ⓓ Ⓔ | 26 Ⓐ Ⓑ Ⓒ Ⓓ Ⓔ | 46 Ⓐ Ⓑ Ⓒ Ⓓ Ⓔ |
| 7 Ⓐ Ⓑ Ⓒ Ⓓ Ⓔ | 27 Ⓐ Ⓑ Ⓒ Ⓓ Ⓔ | 47 Ⓐ Ⓑ Ⓒ Ⓓ Ⓔ |
| 8 Ⓐ Ⓑ Ⓒ Ⓓ Ⓔ | 28 Ⓐ Ⓑ Ⓒ Ⓓ Ⓔ | 48 Ⓐ Ⓑ Ⓒ Ⓓ Ⓔ |
| 9 Ⓐ Ⓑ Ⓒ Ⓓ Ⓔ | 29 Ⓐ Ⓑ Ⓒ Ⓓ Ⓔ | 49 Ⓐ Ⓑ Ⓒ Ⓓ Ⓔ |
| 10 Ⓐ Ⓑ Ⓒ Ⓓ Ⓔ | 30 Ⓐ Ⓑ Ⓒ Ⓓ Ⓔ | 50 Ⓐ Ⓑ Ⓒ Ⓓ Ⓔ |
| 11 Ⓐ Ⓑ Ⓒ Ⓓ Ⓔ | 31 Ⓐ Ⓑ Ⓒ Ⓓ Ⓔ | 51 Ⓐ Ⓑ Ⓒ Ⓓ Ⓔ |
| 12 Ⓐ Ⓑ Ⓒ Ⓓ Ⓔ | 32 Ⓐ Ⓑ Ⓒ Ⓓ Ⓔ | 52 Ⓐ Ⓑ Ⓒ Ⓓ Ⓔ |
| 13 Ⓐ Ⓑ Ⓒ Ⓓ Ⓔ | 33 Ⓐ Ⓑ Ⓒ Ⓓ Ⓔ | 53 Ⓐ Ⓑ Ⓒ Ⓓ Ⓔ |
| 14 Ⓐ Ⓑ Ⓒ Ⓓ Ⓔ | 34 Ⓐ Ⓑ Ⓒ Ⓓ Ⓔ | 54 Ⓐ Ⓑ Ⓒ Ⓓ Ⓔ |
| 15 Ⓐ Ⓑ Ⓒ Ⓓ Ⓔ | 35 Ⓐ Ⓑ Ⓒ Ⓓ Ⓔ | 55 Ⓐ Ⓑ Ⓒ Ⓓ Ⓔ |
| 16 Ⓐ Ⓑ Ⓒ Ⓓ Ⓔ | 36 Ⓐ Ⓑ Ⓒ Ⓓ Ⓔ | 56 Ⓐ Ⓑ Ⓒ Ⓓ Ⓔ |
| 17 Ⓐ Ⓑ Ⓒ Ⓓ Ⓔ | 37 Ⓐ Ⓑ Ⓒ Ⓓ Ⓔ | 57 Ⓐ Ⓑ Ⓒ Ⓓ Ⓔ |
| 18 Ⓐ Ⓑ Ⓒ Ⓓ Ⓔ | 38 Ⓐ Ⓑ Ⓒ Ⓓ Ⓔ | 58 Ⓐ Ⓑ Ⓒ Ⓓ Ⓔ |
| 19 Ⓐ Ⓑ Ⓒ Ⓓ Ⓔ | 39 Ⓐ Ⓑ Ⓒ Ⓓ Ⓔ | 59 Ⓐ Ⓑ Ⓒ Ⓓ Ⓔ |
| 20 Ⓐ Ⓑ Ⓒ Ⓓ Ⓔ | 40 Ⓐ Ⓑ Ⓒ Ⓓ Ⓔ | 60 Ⓐ Ⓑ Ⓒ Ⓓ Ⓔ |

1) When a number is subtracted from 24 and the difference is divided by that number, the result is 3. What is the value of the number?
   A. 2
   B. 4
   C. 6
   D. 12
   E. 24

2) An angle is equal to one fifth of its supplement. What is the measure of that angle?
   A. 20
   B. 30
   C. 45
   D. 60
   E. 90

3) Which of the following is one solution of this equation?
$$x^2 + 2x - 5 = 0$$
   A. $\sqrt{6} - 1$
   B. $\sqrt{2} + 1$
   C. $\sqrt{6} + 1$
   D. $\sqrt{2} - 1$
   E. $\sqrt{12}$

4) Simplify $\frac{4-3i}{-4i}$ ?
   A. $\frac{3}{4} + i$
   B. $\frac{3}{4} - i$
   C. $\frac{1}{4} - i$
   D. $\frac{1}{4} + i$
   E. $i$

$$4x^2 + 6x - 3 \ , \ \ 3x^2 - 5x + 8$$

5) Which of the following is the sum of the two polynomials shown above?
   A. $5x^2 + 3x + 4$
   B. $4x^2 - 6x + 3$
   C. $7x^2 + x + 5$
   D. $7x^2 + 5x + 1$
   E. $x^2 + 5x + 4$

| $x$ | 1 | 2 | 3 |
|---|---|---|---|
| $g(x)$ | $-1$ | $-3$ | $-5$ |

6) The table above shows some values of linear function $g(x)$. Which of the following defines $g(x)$?

A. $g(x) = 2x + 1$
B. $g(x) = 2x - 1$
C. $g(x) = -2x + 1$
D. $g(x) = x + 2$
E. $g(x) = 2x + 2$

7) Right triangle $ABC$ has two legs of lengths $6\ cm$ $(AB)$ and $8\ cm$ $(AC)$. What is the length of the third side $(BC)$?

A.  $4\ cm$
B.  $6\ cm$
C.  $8\ cm$
D.  $10\ cm$
E.  $20\ cm$

8) Which of the following expressions is equal to $\sqrt{\dfrac{x^2}{2} + \dfrac{x^2}{16}}$?

A.  $x$
B.  $\dfrac{3x}{4}$
C.  $x\sqrt{x}$
D.  $\dfrac{x\sqrt{x}}{4}$
E.  $4x$

9) What is the $y-$intercept of the line with the equation $x - 3y = 12$?

A.  1
B.  $-2$
C.  3
D.  $-4$
E.  5

10) If $4a - 3 = 14$ what is the value of $6a$?

A.  5
B.  15
C.  30
D.  45
E.  50

11) Two third of 18 is equal to $\frac{2}{5}$ of what number?

   A. 12
   B. 20
   C. 30
   D. 60
   E. 90

12) The marked price of a computer is $D$ dollar. Its price decreased by 20% in January and later increased by 10% in February. What is the final price of the computer in $D$ dollar?

   A. $0.80\ D$
   B. $0.88\ D$
   C. $0.90\ D$
   D. $1.20\ D$
   E. $1.40\ D$

13) If $x \neq 0$ and $x = x^{-6}$, what is the value of $x$?

   A. $-2$
   B. 1
   C. 2
   D. 3
   E. 4

14) Which of the following is equal to expression $\frac{5}{x^2} + \frac{7x-3}{x^3}$ ?

   A. $\dfrac{6x+1}{x^3}$
   B. $\dfrac{10x+6}{x^3}$
   C. $\dfrac{12x+}{x^3}$
   D. $\dfrac{13x+2}{x^3}$
   E. $\dfrac{6x+4}{x^3}$

15) Which of the following is the equation of a quadratic graph with a vertex $(3, -3)$?

   A. $y = 3x^2 - 3$
   B. $y = -3x^2 + 3$
   C. $y = x^2 + 3x - 3$
   D. $y = 4(x - 3)^2 - 3$
   E. $y = 4x^2 + 3x - 3$

16) A boat sails 40 miles south and then 30 miles east. How far is the boat from its start point?
   A. 45 $miles$
   B. 50 $miles$
   C. 60 $miles$
   D. 70 $miles$
   E. 80 $miles$

17) What is the average of $4x + 2, -6x - 5$ and $8x + 2$?
   A. $3x + 2$
   B. $3x - 2$
   C. $2x + 1$
   D. $2x - \frac{1}{3}$
   E. $x - \frac{1}{3}$

18) The score of Emma was half as that of Ava and the score of Mia was twice that of Ava. If the score of Mia was 60, what is the score of Emma?
   A. 12
   B. 15
   C. 20
   D. 30
   E. 40

19) The average of five consecutive numbers is 38. What is the smallest number?
   A. 38
   B. 36
   C. 34
   D. 12
   E. 8

20) Tickets to a movie cost $12.50 for adults and $7.50 for students. A group of 12 friends purchased tickets for $125. How many student tickets did they buy?
   A. 3
   B. 5
   C. 7
   D. 8
   E. 9

21) If the ratio of $5a$ to $2b$ is $\frac{1}{10}$, what is the ratio of $a$ to $b$?

   A.  10

   B.  25

   C.  $\frac{1}{25}$

   D.  $\frac{1}{20}$

   E.  $\frac{1}{10}$

22) A chemical solution contains 4% alcohol. If there is $24\ ml$ of alcohol, what is the volume of the solution?

   A.  $240\ ml$

   B.  $480\ ml$

   C.  $600\ ml$

   D.  $1,200\ ml$

   E.  $2,400\ ml$

23) The average weight of 18 girls in a class is $60\ kg$ and the average weight of 32 boys in the same class is $62\ kg$. What is the average weight of all the 50 students in that class?

   A.  60

   B.  61.28

   C.  61.68

   D.  61.90

   E.  62.20

24) If $x = 9$, what is the value of $y$ in the following equation? $2y = \frac{2x^2}{3} + 6$

   A.  30

   B.  45

   C.  60

   D.  120

   E.  180

25) Sara orders a box of pen for $3 per box. A tax of 8.5% is added to the cost of the pens before a flat shipping fee of $6 closest out the transaction. Which of the following represents total cost of $p$ boxes of pens in dollars?

   A.  $1.085(3p) + 6$

   B.  $6p + 3$

   C.  $1.085(6p) + 3$

   D.  $3p + 6$

   E.  $p + 6$

26) The average of $13, 15, 20$ and $x$ is 18. What is the value of $x$?
   A. 9
   B. 15
   C. 18
   D. 20
   E. 24

27) The price of a sofa is decreased by 25% to $420. What was its original price?
   A. $480
   B. $520
   C. $560
   D. $600
   E. $800

28) A bank is offering 4.5% simple interest on a savings account. If you deposit $8,000, how much interest will you earn in five years?
   A. $360
   B. $720
   C. $1,800
   D. $3,600
   E. $4,800

29) Multiply and write the product in scientific notation: $(4.2 \times 10^6) \times (2.6 \times 10^{-5})$
   A. $1092 \times 10$
   B. $10.92 \times 10^6$
   C. $109.2 \times 10^{-5}$
   D. $10.92 \times 10^{11}$
   E. $1.092 \times 10^2$

30) A plant grows at a linear rate. After 3 weeks, the plant is 45 cm tall. Which of the following functions represents the relationship between the height $(y)$ of the plant and number of weeks of growth $(x)$?
   A. $y(x) = 40x + 8$
   B. $y(x) = 25x + 40$
   C. $y(x) = 20x$
   D. $y(x) = 15x$
   E. $y(x) = 3x$

31) Solve for $x$: $4(x + 1) = 6(x - 4) + 20$
   A. 12
   B. 8
   C. 6.2
   D. 5.5
   E. 4

32) Which of the following expressions is equivalent to $2x(4 + 2y)$?

   A.  $2xy + 8x$
   B.  $8xy + 8x$
   C.  $xy + 8$
   D.  $2xy + 8x$
   E.  $4xy + 8x$

33) If $y = 4ab + 3b^3$, what is y when $a = 2$ and $b = 3$?

   A.  24
   B.  31
   C.  36
   D.  51
   E.  105

34) If $x \begin{bmatrix} 2 & 0 \\ 0 & 4 \end{bmatrix} = \begin{bmatrix} x + 3y - 5 & 0 \\ 0 & 2y + 10 \end{bmatrix}$, what is the product of $x$ and $y$?

   A.  1
   B.  2
   C.  10
   D.  11
   E.  12

35) If $f(x) = 3^x$ and $g(x) = log_3 x$, which of the following expressions is equal to $f(3g(p))$?

   A.  $3P$
   B.  $3^p$
   C.  $p^3$
   D.  $p^9$
   E.  $\frac{p}{3}$

36) The following table represents the value of $x$ and function $f(x)$. Which of the following could be the equation of the function $f(x)$?

   A. $f(x) = x^2 - 5$
   B. $f(x) = x^2 - 1$
   C. $f(x) = \sqrt{x + 2}$
   D. $f(x) = \sqrt{x} + 4$
   E. $f(x) = \sqrt{x} + 6$

| $x$ | $f(x)$ |
|---|---|
| 1 | 5 |
| 4 | 6 |
| 9 | 7 |
| 16 | 8 |

37) Which of the following points lies on the line $2x + 4y = 10$
   A. $(2, 1)$
   B. $(-1, 3)$
   C. $(-2, 2)$
   D. $(2, 2)$
   E. $(2, 8)$

38) Which graph shows a non-proportional linear relationship between $x$ and $y$?

☐ A.

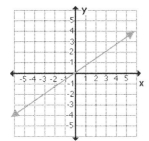

☐ B.

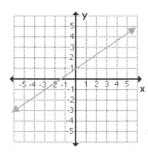

☐ C.

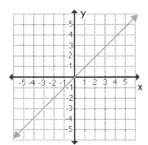

☐ D.

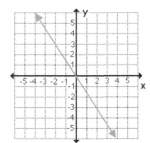

39) A ladder leans against a wall forming a $60°$ angle between the ground and the ladder. If the bottom of the ladder is 30 feet away from the wall, how long is the ladder?
   A. $30\ feet$
   B. $40\ feet$
   C. $50\ feet$
   D. $60\ feet$
   E. $120\ feet$

40) Right triangle $ABC$ is shown below. Which of the following is true for all possible values of angle $A$ and $B$?

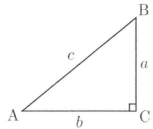

   A. $tan\ A\ =\ tan\ B$

   B. $sin\ A\ =\ cos\ B$

   C. $tan^2 A = tan^2 B$

   D. $tan\ A = 1$

   E. $cot\ A = sinB$

41) If $x + y = 0,\ 4x - 2y = 24$, which of the following ordered pairs $(x, y)$ satisfies both equations?
   A. $(4, 3)$
   B. $(5, 4)$
   C. $(4, -4)$
   D. $(4, -6)$
   E. $(2, -6)$

42) If $f(x) = 3x + 4(x + 1) + 2$ then $f(3x) =$?
   A. $21x + 6$
   B. $16x - 6$
   C. $25x + 4$
   D. $12x + 3$
   E. $2x + 3$

43) A line in the $xy$-plane passes through origin and has a slope of $\frac{2}{3}$. Which of the following points lies on the line?
   A. $(2,1)$
   B. $(4,1)$
   C. $(9,6)$
   D. $(9,3)$
   E. $(6,-3)$

44) Which of the following is equivalent to $(3n^2 + 4n + 6) - (2n^2 - 5)$?
   A. $n + 4n^2$
   B. $n^2 - 3$
   C. $n^2 + 4n + 11$
   D. $n + 2$
   E. $n - 2$

45) If $(ax + 4)(bx + 3) = 10x^2 + cx + 12$ for all values of $x$ and $a + b = 7$, what are the two possible values for $c$?

   A. $22, 21$

   B. $20, 22$

   C. $23, 26$

   D. $24, 23$

   E. $24, 26$

46) If $x \neq -4$ and $x \neq 6$, which of the following is equivalent to $\dfrac{1}{\frac{1}{x-6}+\frac{1}{x+4}}$?

   A. $\dfrac{(x-6)(x+4)}{(x-6)+(x+4)}$

   B. $\dfrac{(x+4)+(x-6)}{(x+4)(x-6)}$

   C. $\dfrac{(x+4)(x-6)}{(x+4)-(x+6)}$

   D. $\dfrac{(x+4)+(x-6)}{(x+4)-(x-6)}$

   E. $\dfrac{(x-4)+(x-6)}{(x+4)-(x-6)}$

$$y < a - x, y > x + b$$

47) In the $xy$-plane, if $(0,0)$ is a solution to the system of inequalities above, which of the following relationships between $a$ and $b$ must be true?

   A. $a < b$

   B. $a > b$

   C. $a = b$

   D. $a = b + a$

   E. $a = b - a$

48) Which of the following points lies on the line that goes through the points $(2,4)$ and $(4,5)$?

   A. $(9,9)$

   B. $(9,6)$

   C. $(6,9)$

   D. $(6,6)$

   E. $(0,6)$

49) Calculate $f(4)$ for the following function $f$.
$$f(x) = x^2 - 3x$$
    A.  0

    B.  4

    C.  12

    D.  20

    E.  24

50) John buys a pepper plant that is 6 inches tall. With regular watering the plant grows 4 inches a year. Writing John's plant's height as a function of time, what does the $y$ −intercept represent?
    A.  The $y$ −intercept represents the rate of grows of the plant which is 4 inches
    B.  The $y$ −intercept represents the starting height of 6 inches
    C.  The $y$ −intercept represents the rate of growth of plant which is 4 inches per year
    D.  The $y$ −intercept is zero
    E.  There is no $y$ −intercept

51) If $\dfrac{3}{x} = \dfrac{12}{x-9}$ what is the value of $\dfrac{x}{6}$?
    A.  $-2$
    B.  $2$
    C.  $-\dfrac{1}{2}$
    D.  $\dfrac{1}{2}$
    E.  $0$

52) Which of the following is an equation of a circle in the $xy$-plane with center $(0, 4)$ and a radius with endpoint $(\frac{5}{3}, 6)$?
    A.  $(x + 1)^2 + (y - 4)^2 = \dfrac{61}{9}$
    B.  $2x^2 + (y + 4)^2 = \dfrac{61}{9}$
    C.  $(x - 2)^2 + (y - 4)^2 = \dfrac{61}{9}$
    D.  $x^2 + (y - 4)^2 = \dfrac{61}{9}$
    E.  $x^2 + (y - 4)^2 = 25$

53) Given a right triangle $\Delta ABC$ whose $n\angle B = 90°$, $\sin C = \frac{2}{3}$, find $\cos A$?

    A.  1

    B.  $\frac{1}{2}$

    C.  $\frac{2}{3}$

    D.  $\frac{3}{2}$

    E.  $\frac{5}{2}$

54) What is the equation of the following graph?

    A.  $x^2 + 6x + 5$

    B.  $x^2 + 2x + 4$

    C.  $2x^2 - 4x + 4$

    D.  $2x^2 + 4x + 2$

    E.  $4x^2 + 2x + 3$

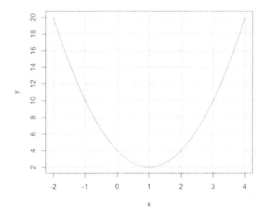

55) In the $xy-$plane, the line determined by the points $(6, m)$ and $(m, 12)$ passes through the origin. Which of the following could be the value of $m$?

    A.  $\sqrt{6}$

    B.  12

    C.  $6\sqrt{2}$

    D.  9

    E.  6

56) A function $g(3) = 5$ and $g(6) = 4$. A function $f(5) = 2$ and $f(4) = 7$. What is the value of $f(g(6))$?

    A.  5

    B.  7

    C.  8

    D.  9

    E.  12

57) What is the area of the following equilateral triangle if the side $AB = 8\ cm$?

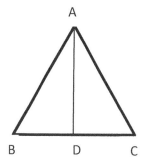

A. $16\sqrt{3}\ cm^2$
B. $8\sqrt{3}\ cm^2$
C. $\sqrt{3}\ cm^2$
D. $8\ cm^2$
E. $6\ cm^2$

58) A function $g(x)$ satisfies $g(4) = 5$ and $g(7) = 8$. A function $f(x)$ satisfies $f(5) = 18$ and $f(8) = 35$. What is the value of $f\big(g(7)\big)$?
   A. 12
   B. 22
   C. 35
   D. 42
   E. 46

$$(x + 2)^2 + (y - 4)^2 = 16$$

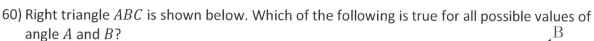

59) In the standard $(x, y)$ coordinate system plane, what is the area of the circle with the above equation?
   A. $24\pi$
   B. $18\pi$
   C. $16\pi$
   D. $\sqrt{10}$
   E. $\sqrt{10}\ \pi$

60) Right triangle $ABC$ is shown below. Which of the following is true for all possible values of angle $A$ and $B$?

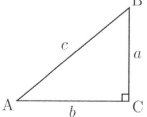

A. $tan\ A = \dfrac{a}{c}$
B. $sin\ A = \dfrac{a}{c}$
C. $cot^2 A = 0$
D. $tan\ A = 1$
E. $cos\ A = \dfrac{b}{a}$

## End of CLEP College Algebra Practice Test 2

# CLEP College Algebra Practice Tests Answer Keys

Now, it's time to review your results to see where you went wrong and what areas you need to improve.

| CLEP College Algebra Practice Test 1 | | | | | | CLEP College Algebra Practice Test 2 | | | | | |
|---|---|---|---|---|---|---|---|---|---|---|---|
| 1 | A | 21 | E | 41 | D | 1 | C | 21 | C | 41 | C |
| 2 | A | 22 | E | 42 | C | 2 | B | 22 | C | 42 | A |
| 3 | D | 23 | B | 43 | B | 3 | A | 23 | B | 43 | C |
| 4 | D | 24 | A | 44 | C | 4 | A | 24 | A | 44 | C |
| 5 | B | 25 | D | 45 | C | 5 | C | 25 | A | 45 | C |
| 6 | C | 26 | A | 46 | D | 6 | C | 26 | E | 46 | A |
| 7 | C | 27 | E | 47 | A | 7 | D | 27 | C | 47 | B |
| 8 | C | 28 | B | 48 | D | 8 | B | 28 | C | 48 | D |
| 9 | B | 29 | C | 49 | D | 9 | D | 29 | E | 49 | B |
| 10 | D | 30 | D | 50 | D | 10 | C | 30 | D | 50 | B |
| 11 | D | 31 | A | 51 | C | 11 | C | 31 | E | 51 | C |
| 12 | A | 32 | A | 52 | C | 12 | B | 32 | E | 52 | D |
| 13 | C | 33 | C | 53 | B | 13 | B | 33 | E | 53 | C |
| 14 | B | 34 | E | 54 | B | 14 | C | 34 | E | 54 | C |
| 15 | B | 35 | E | 55 | A | 15 | D | 35 | C | 55 | C |
| 16 | B | 36 | B | 56 | D | 16 | B | 36 | D | 56 | B |
| 17 | D | 37 | E | 57 | B | 17 | D | 37 | B | 57 | A |
| 18 | A | 38 | D | 58 | A | 18 | B | 38 | B | 58 | C |
| 19 | B | 39 | C | 59 | A | 19 | B | 39 | D | 59 | C |
| 20 | E | 40 | A | 60 | D | 20 | B | 40 | B | 60 | B |

# CLEP College Algebra Practice Tests

# Answers and Explanations

## CLEP College Algebra Practice Test 1

**1) Choice A is correct**

$(\frac{f}{g})(x) = \frac{f(x)}{g(x)} = \frac{2x+2}{x^2+4x}$

**2) Choice A is correct.**

The equation of a line is: $y = mx + b$, where $m$ is the slope and $b$ is the y-intercept.

First find the slope: $m = \frac{y_2-y_1}{x_2-x_1} = \frac{15-(-5)}{8-3} = \frac{20}{5} = 4$. Then, we have: $y = 4x + b$

Choose one point and plug in the values of $x$ and $y$ in the equation to solve for $b$.

Let's choose the point $(3, -5)$. $y = 4x + b \rightarrow -5 = 4(3) + b \rightarrow -5 = 12 + b \rightarrow b = -17$

The equation of the line is: $y = 4x - 17$

**3) Choice D is correct**

Use FOIL method. $(5x + 2y)(2x - y) = 10x^2 - 5xy + 4xy - 2y^2 = 10x^2 - xy - 2y^2$

**4) Choice D is correct**

To solve absolute values equations, write two equations. $x - 10$ could be positive 4, or negative 4. Therefore, $x - 10 = 4 \Rightarrow x = 14$, $x - 10 = -4 \Rightarrow x = 6$. Find the product of solutions: $6 \times 14 = 84$

**5) Choice B is correct**

The equation of a line in slope intercept form is: $y = mx + b$. Solve for $y$.

$4x - 2y = 6 \Rightarrow -2y = 6 - 4x \Rightarrow y = (6 - 4x) \div (-2) \Rightarrow y = 2x - 3$. The slope is 2.

The slope of the line perpendicular to this line is: $m_1 \times m_2 = -1 \Rightarrow 2 \times m_2 = -1 \Rightarrow m_2 = -\frac{1}{2}$.

**6) Choice C is correct**

Plug in the value of $x$ and $y$. $x = 3$ and $y = -2$.

**7) Choice C is correct**

To rewrite $\frac{2+3i}{5-2i}$ in the standard form $a+bi$, multiply the numerator and denominator of $\frac{2+3i}{5-2i}$ by the conjugate, $5+2i$. This gives $\left(\frac{2+3i}{5-2i}\right)\left(\frac{5+2i}{5+2i}\right) = \frac{10+4i+15i+6i^2}{5^2-(2i)^2}$. Since $i^2 = -1$, this last fraction can be rewritten as $\frac{10+4i+15i+\ (-1)}{25-4(-1)} = \frac{4+19i}{29}$.

**8) Choice C is correct**

First find the value of $b$, and then find $f(3)$. Since $f(2) = 35$, substuting 2 for $x$ and 35 for $f(x)$ gives $35 = b(2)^2 + 15 = 4b + 15$. Solving this equation gives $b = 5$. Thus

$$f(x) = 5x^2 + 15, \quad f(3) = 5(3)^2 + 15 \rightarrow f(3) = 45 + 15, \quad f(3) = 60$$

**9) Choice B is correct**

The diagonal of the square is 4. Let $x$ be the side. Use Pythagorean Theorem: $a^2 + b^2 = c^2$

$$x^2 + x^2 = 4^2 \Rightarrow 2x^2 = 4^2 \Rightarrow 2x^2 = 16 \Rightarrow x^2 = 8 \Rightarrow x = \sqrt{8}$$

The area of the square is: $\sqrt{8} \times \sqrt{8} = 8$

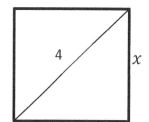

**10) Choice D is correct**

Solve for the sum of five numbers.

$$\text{average} = \frac{\text{sum of terms}}{\text{number of terms}} \Rightarrow 26 = \frac{\text{sum of 5 numbers}}{5} \Rightarrow \text{sum of 5 numbers} = 26 \times 5 = 130$$

The sum of 5 numbers is 130. If a sixth number 42 is added, then the sum of 6 numbers is

$130 + 42 = 172$. The new average is: $\frac{\text{sum of 6 numbers}}{6} = \frac{172}{6} = 28.66$

**11) Choice D is correct**

The rate of construction company $= \frac{30 \text{ cm}}{1 \text{ min}} = 30$ cm/min

Height of the wall after 40 minutes $= \frac{30 \text{ cm}}{1 \text{ min}} \times 40 \text{ min} = 1200$ cm

Let $x$ be the height of wall, then $\frac{3}{4}x = 1200$ cm $\rightarrow x = \frac{4 \times 1200}{3} \rightarrow x = 1600$ cm $= 16\ m$

**12) Choice A is correct**

$x - 2 \geq 3 \rightarrow x \geq 3 + 2 \rightarrow x \geq 5$ Or $x - 2 \leq -3 \rightarrow x \leq -3 + 2 \rightarrow x \leq -1$

Then, solution is: $x \geq 5 \cup x \leq -1$

**13) Choice C is correct**

When 5 times the number $x$ is added to 10, the result is $10 + 5x$. Since this result is equal to 35, the equation $10 + 5x = 35$ is true. Subtracting 10 from each side of $10 + 5x = 35$ gives $5x = 25$, and then dividing both sides by 5 gives $x = 5$. Therefore, 3 times $x$ added to 6, or $6 + 3x$, is equal to $6 + 3(5) = 21$.

**14) Choice B is correct**

Fining $g$ in term of $h$, simply means "solve the equation for $g$". To solve for $g$, isolate it on one side of the equation. Since $g$ is on the left-hand side, just keep it there.

Subtract both sides by $3h$.     $3h + g - 3h = 8h + 4 - 3h$

And simplifying makes the equation $g = 5h + 4$, which happens to be the answer.

**15) Choice B is correct**

Isolate and solve for $x$. $\frac{2}{3}x + \frac{1}{6} = \frac{1}{2} \Rightarrow \frac{2}{3}x = \frac{1}{2} - \frac{1}{6} = \frac{1}{3} \Rightarrow \frac{2}{3}x = \frac{1}{3}$ .Multiply both sides by the reciprocal of the coefficient of $x$. $(\frac{3}{2}) \frac{2}{3}x = \frac{1}{3}(\frac{3}{2}) \Rightarrow x = \frac{3}{6} = \frac{1}{2}$

**16) Choice B is correct**

Use simple interest formula: $I = prt$ ($I$ = interest, $p$ = principal, $r$ = rate, $t$ = time).

$$I = (12{,}000)(0.045)(2) = 1{,}080$$

**17) Choice D is correct**

Simplify. $7x^2y^3(2x^2y)^3 = 7x^2y^3(8x^6y^3) = 56x^8y^6$

**18) Choice E is correct**

Frist factor the function: $f(x) = x^3 + 7x^2 + 12x = x\,(x + 3)(x + 4)$

To find the zeros, $f(x)$ should be zero. $f(x) = x\,(x + 3)(x + 4) = 0$

Therefore, the zeros are: $x = 0$,     $(x + 3) = 0 \Rightarrow x = -3$,     $(x + 4) = 0 \Rightarrow x = -4$

**19) Choice B is correct.**

$sin^2a + cos^2a = 1$, then: $x + 1 = 3$,     $x = 2$

**20) Choice E is correct.**

Solve for $x$. $\sqrt{3x} = \sqrt{y}$. Square both sides of the equation: $(\sqrt{3x})^2 = (\sqrt{y})^2 \rightarrow 3x = y \rightarrow x = \frac{y}{3}$

**21) Choice E is correct**

$g(x) = -4$, then $f\big(g(x)\big) = f(-4) = 2\,(-4)^3 + 5(-4)^2 + 2(-4) = -128 + 80 - 8 = -56$

**22) Choice E is correct**

Use the information provided in the question to draw the shape.

Use Pythagorean Theorem: $a^2 + b^2 = c^2$

$50^2 + 120^2 = c^2 \Rightarrow 2,500 + 14,400 = c^2 \Rightarrow$

$16,900 = c^2 \Rightarrow c = 130$

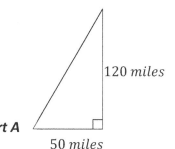

120 *miles*

**Port A**

50 *miles*

**23) Choice B is correct**

Plug in 104 for $F$ and then solve for $C$.

$C = \dfrac{5}{9}\,(F - 32) \Rightarrow C = \dfrac{5}{9}\,(104 - 32) \Rightarrow C = \dfrac{5}{9}\,(72) = 40$

**24) Choice A is correct**

The width of the rectangle is twice its length. Let $x$ be the length. Then, $width = 2x$

Perimeter of the rectangle is $2\,(width + length) = 2(2x + x) = 72 \Rightarrow 6x = 72 \Rightarrow x = 12$. Length of the rectangle is 12 meters.

**25) Choice D is correct**

$average = \dfrac{\text{sum of terms}}{\text{number of terms}} \Rightarrow$ (average of 6 numbers) $14 = \dfrac{\text{sum of numbers}}{6} \Rightarrow$ sum of 6 numbers is $14 \times 6 = 84$, (average of 4 numbers) $10 = \dfrac{\text{sum of numbers}}{4} \Rightarrow$ sum of 4 numbers is $10 \times 4 = 40$. *sum of 6 numbers $-$ sum of 4 numbers $=$ sum of 2 numbers*,

$84 - 40 = 44$ average of 2 numbers $= \dfrac{44}{2} = 22$

**26) Choice A is correct**

First, find the number. Let $x$ be the number. Write the equation and solve for $x$. 150% of a number is 75, then: $1.5 \times x = 75 \Rightarrow x = 75 \div 1.5 = 50$, 80% of 50 is: $0.8 \times 50 = 40$

**27) Choice E is correct**

Solve for $y$. $4x - 2y = 12 \Rightarrow -2y = 12 - 4x \Rightarrow y = 2x - 6$. The slope of the line is 2.

**28) Choice B is correct**

the population is increased by 10% and 20%. 10% increase changes the population to 110% of original population. For the second increase, multiply the result by 120%.

$(1.10) \times (1.20) = 1.32 = 132\%$. 32 percent of the population is increased after two years.

**29) Choice C is correct**

The formula for the area of the circle is: $A = \pi r^2$ ,The area is $36\pi$. Therefore:$A = \pi r^2 \Rightarrow 6\pi = \pi r^2$, Divide both sides by $\pi$: $36 = r^2 \Rightarrow r = 6$. Diameter of a circle is $2 \times$ radius. Then:

$$Diameter = 2 \times 6 = 12$$

**30) Choice D is correct**

If 20% of a number is 4, what is the number: $20\% \ of \ x = 4 \Rightarrow 0.20 \ x = 4 \Rightarrow x = 4 \div 0.20 = 20$

**31) Choice A is correct**

Substituting $x$ for $y$ in first equation. $5x + 2y = 3$, $5x + 2(x) = 3$, $\qquad 7x = 3$

Divide both side of $7x = 3$ by 3 gives $x = \dfrac{3}{7}$

**32) Choice A is correct**

There are 5 floors, $x$ rooms in each floor, and $y$ chairs per room. If you multiply 5 floors by $x$, there are $5x$ rooms in the hotel. To get the number of chairs in the hotel, multiply $5x$ by $y$. $5xy$ is the number of chairs in the hotel.

**33) Choice C is correct**

If $\beta = 3\gamma$, then multiplying both sides by 12 gives $12\beta = 36\gamma$.

$\alpha = 2\beta$, thus $\alpha = 6\gamma$. Multiply both sides of the equation by 6 gives $6\alpha = 36\gamma$.

**34) Choice E is correct**

$$g(x) = -3, \text{ then } f\big(g(x)\big) = f(-3) = 2 \, (-3)^3 + 5(-3)^2 + 2(-3) = -54 + 45 - 6 = -15$$

**35) Choice E is correct**

Let $x$ be the width of the rectangle. Use Pythagorean Theorem:

$$a^2 + b^2 = c^2$$

$$x^{\,2} + 6^{\,2} = 10^{\,2} \Rightarrow x^{\,2} + 36 = 100 \Rightarrow x^{\,2} = 100 - 36 = 64 \Rightarrow x = 8$$

Perimeter of the rectangle $= \ 2 \, (length \ + \ width) = \ 2 \, (8 \ + \ 6) = \ 2 \, (14) \ = 28$

**36) Choice B is correct**

The perimeter of the trapezoid is 40.herefore, the missing side (height) is

$= 40 - 8 - 12 - 6 = 14$. Area of a trapezoid: $A \ = \ \frac{1}{2} \ h \, (b_1 \ + \ b_2) \ = \ \frac{1}{2} \, (14) \, (6 + 8) \ = 98$

**37) Choice E is correct**

$$f\big(g(x)\big) = 2 \times (\frac{1}{x})^3 + 2 = \frac{2}{x^3} + 2$$

**38)  Choice D is correct**

Use the information provided in the question to draw the shape.

Use Pythagorean Theorem: $a^2 + b^2 = c^2$

$80^2 + 150^2 = c^2 \Rightarrow 6400 + 22500 = c^2 \Rightarrow 28900 = c^2 \Rightarrow c = 170$

*1500 miles*

*Port A*

*80 miles*

**39)  Choice C is correct**

Write the ratio of $5a$ to $2b$. $\frac{5a}{2b} = \frac{1}{10}$. Use cross multiplication and then simplify.

$$5a \times 10 = 2b \times 1 \rightarrow 50a = 2b \rightarrow a = \frac{2b}{50} = \frac{b}{25}$$

Now, find the ratio of $a$ to $b$. $\frac{a}{b} = \frac{\frac{b}{25}}{b} \rightarrow \frac{b}{25} \div b = \frac{b}{25} \times \frac{1}{b} = \frac{b}{25b} = \frac{1}{25}$

**40)  Choice A is correct**

Plug in the value of $x$ in the equation and solve for $y$. $2y = \frac{2x^2}{3} + 6 \rightarrow 2y = \frac{2(9)^2}{3} + 6 \rightarrow$

$$2y = \frac{2(81)}{3} + 6 \rightarrow 2y = 54 + 6 = 60 \rightarrow 2y = 60 \rightarrow y = 30$$

**41) Choice D is correct**

Since $N = 6$, substitute 6 for $N$ in the equation $\frac{x-3}{5} = N$, which gives $\frac{x-3}{5} = 6$. Multiplying both sides of $\frac{x-3}{5} = 6$ by 5 gives $x - 3 = 30$ and then adding 3 to both sides of $x - 3 = 30$ then, $x = 33$.

**42) Choice C is correct**

$b^{\frac{m}{n}} = \sqrt[n]{b^m}$ For any positive integers $m$ and $n$. Thus, $b^{\frac{3}{5}} = \sqrt[5]{b^3}$

**43) Choice B is correct**

The total number of pages read by Sara is 3 (hours she spent reading) multiplied by her rate of reading: $\frac{N pages}{hour} \times 3 hours = 3N$

Similarly, the total number of pages read by Mary is 4 (hours she spent reading) multiplied by her rate of reading: $\frac{M pages}{hour} \times 4 hours = 4M$ the total number of pages read by Sara and Mary is the sum of the total number of pages read by Sara and the total number of pages read by Mary: $3N + 4M$.

**44) Choice C is correct**

We know that: $i = \sqrt{-1} \Rightarrow i^2 = -1$

$(-4 + 9i)(3 + 5i) = -12 - 20i + 27i + 45i^2 = -12 + 7i - 45 = -57 + 7i$

**45) Choice C is correct**

First find the value of $b$, and then find $f(5)$. Since $f(2) = 35$, substuting 2 for $x$ and 35 for $f(x)$ gives $35 = b(2)^2 + 15 = 4b + 15$. Solving this equation gives $b = 5$. Thus

$f(x) = 5x^2 + 15, \quad f(5) = 5(5)^2 + 15 \rightarrow f(5) = 125 + 15, \quad f(3) = 140$

**46) Choice D is correct**

Solving Systems of Equations by Elimination: Multiply the first equation by $(-2)$, then add it to the second equation.

$$\begin{array}{l} -2(2x + 5y = 11) \\ \underline{4x - 2y = -14} \end{array} \Rightarrow \begin{array}{l} -4x - 10y = -22 \\ 4x - 2y = -14 \end{array} \Rightarrow -12y = -36 \Rightarrow y = 3$$

Plug in the value of $y$ into one of the equations and solve for $x$.

$2x + 5(3) = 11 \Rightarrow 2x + 15 = 11 \Rightarrow 2x = -4 \Rightarrow x = -2$

**47) Choice A is correct**

Identify the input value. Since the function is in the form $f(x)$ and the question asks to calculate $f(4)$, the input value is four. $f(4) \rightarrow x = 4$, Using the function, input the desired $x$ value. Now substitute 4 in for every $x$ in the function. $f(x) = 3x^2 - 4$, $f(4) = 3(4)^2 - 4$, $f(4) = 48 - 4$, $f(4) = 44$

**48) Choice D is correct**

Frist factor the function: $f(x) = x^3 + 5x^2 + 6x = x(x + 2)(x + 3)$, To find the zeros, $f(x)$ should be zero. $f(x) = x(x + 2)(x + 3) = 0$, Therefore, the zeros are: $x = 0$, $(x + 2) = 0 \Rightarrow x = -2$, $(x + 3) = 0 \Rightarrow x = -3$

**49) Choice D is correct**

To simplify the fraction, multiply both numerator and denominator by $i$.

$\frac{4-3i}{-4i} \times \frac{i}{i} = \frac{4i-3i^2}{-4i^2}, i^2 - 1$, Then: $\frac{4i-3i^2}{-4i^2} = \frac{4i-3(-1)}{-4(-1)} = \frac{4i+3}{4} = \frac{4i}{4} + \frac{3}{4} = \frac{3}{4} + i$

**50) Choice D is correct**

The $x$-intercepts of the parabola represented by $y = x^2 - 7x + 12$ in the $xy$-plane are the values of $x$ for which $y$ is equal to 0.

The factored form of the equation, $y = (x - 3)(x - 4)$, shows that $y$ equals 0 if and only if

$x = 3$ or $x = 4$. Thus, the factored form $y = (x - 3)(x - 4)$, displays the $x$-intercepts. of the parabola as the constants 3 and 4.

**51) Choice C is correct**

If $x - a$ is a factor of $g(x)$, then $g(a)$ must equal 0. Based on the table $g(2) = 0$. Therefore, $x - 2$ must be a factor of $g(x)$.

**52) Choice C is correct**

To solve this problem first solve the equation for $c$. $\frac{c}{b} = 2$

Multiply by $b$ on both sides. Then: $b \times \frac{c}{b} = 2 \times b \rightarrow c = 2b$.     Now to calculate $\frac{4b}{c}$, substitute the value for $c$ into the denominator and simplify. $\frac{4b}{c} = \frac{4b}{2b} = \frac{4}{2} = \frac{2}{1} = 2$

**53) Choice B is correct**

$x + 5 = 8 \rightarrow x = 8 - 5 = 3, 2y - 1 = 5 \rightarrow 2y = 6 \rightarrow y = 3, xy + 15 = 3 \times 3 + 15 = 24$

**54) Choice B is correct**

The equation $\frac{a-b}{b} = \frac{10}{13}$ can be rewritten as $\frac{a}{b} - \frac{b}{b} = \frac{10}{13}$, from which it follows that $\frac{a}{b} - 1 = \frac{10}{13}$, or $\frac{a}{b} = \frac{10}{13} + 1 = \frac{23}{13}$.

**55) Choice A is correct**

First write the equation in slope intercept form. Add $2x$ to both sides to get $6y = 2x + 24$. Now divide both sides by 6 to get $y = \frac{1}{3}x + 4$. The slope of this line is $\frac{1}{3}$, so any line that also has a slope of $\frac{1}{3}$ would be parallel to it. Only choice A has a slope of $\frac{1}{3}$.

**56) Choice D is correct**

$$average = \frac{sum\ of\ terms}{number\ of\ terms} \Rightarrow 20 = \frac{13 + 15 + 20 + x}{4} \Rightarrow 80 = 48 + x \Rightarrow x = 32$$

**57) Choice B is correct**

$\frac{x}{3+4} = \frac{y}{11-8} \rightarrow \frac{x}{7} = \frac{y}{3} \rightarrow 7y = 3x \rightarrow y = \frac{3}{7}x$

**58) Choice A is correct**

The sum of all angles in a quadrilateral is 360 degrees. Let $x$ be the smallest angle in the quadrilateral. Then the angles are: $x, 2x, 3x, 4x$,

$x + 2x + 3x + 4x = 360 \rightarrow 10x = 360 \rightarrow x = 36$, The angles in the quadrilateral are: $36°, 72°, 108°$, and $144°$, The smallest angle is 36 degrees.

**59) Choice A is correct**

Since a box of pen costs \$3, then $3p$ Represents the cost of $p$ boxes of pen. Multiplying this number times 1.085 will increase the cost by the 8.5% for tax. Then add the \$6 shipping fee for the total: $1.085(3p) + 6$

**60) Choice D is correct**

Rate of change (growth or $x$) is 8 per week. $40 \div 5 = 8$

Since the plant grows at a linear rate, then the relationship between the height $(y)$ of the plant and number of weeks of growth $(x)$ can be written as: $y(x) = 8x$

# CLEP College Algebra Practice Test 2

## 1) Choice C is correct

Let $x$ be the number. Write the equation and solve for $x$. $(24 - x) \div x = 3$. Multiply both sides by $x$. $(24 - x) = 3x$, then add x both sides. $24 = 4x$, now divide both sides by 4. $x = 6$

## 2) Choice B is correct

The sum of supplement angles is 180. Let $x$ be that angle. Therefore, $x + 5x = 180$

$6x = 180$, divide both sides by 6: $x = 30$

## 3) Choice A is correct

$$x1,2 = \frac{-b \pm \sqrt{b^2 - 4ac}}{2a} \qquad ax2 + bx + c = 0$$

$x2 + 2x - 5 = 0 \qquad\qquad \Rightarrow \qquad$ then: a = 1, b = 2 and c = $-5$

$$x = \frac{-2 + \sqrt{2^2 - 4.1.-5}}{2.1} = \sqrt{6} - 1 \qquad x = \frac{-2 - \sqrt{2^2 - 4.1.-5}}{2.1} = -1 - \sqrt{6}$$

## 4) Choice A is correct

*To simplify the fraction, multiply both numerator and denominator by i.*

$$\frac{4-3i}{-4i} \times \frac{i}{i} = \frac{4i - 3i^2}{-4i^2}. \qquad i^2 - 1, \text{ Then: } \frac{4i - 3i^2}{-4i^2} = \frac{4i - 3(-1)}{-4(-1)} = \frac{4i+3}{4} = \frac{4i}{4} + \frac{3}{4} = i + \frac{3}{4}$$

## 5) Choice C is correct

The sum of the two polynomials is $(4x^2 + 6x - 3) + (3x^2 - 5x + 8)$

This can be rewritten by combining like terms: $(4x^2 + 6x - 3) + (3x^2 - 5x + 8) = (4x^2 + 3x^2) + (6x - 5x) + (-3 + 8) = 7x^2 + x + 5$

## 6) Choice C is correct

Plugin the values of x in the choices provided. The points are $(1, -1), (2, -3),$ and $(3, -5)$

For $(1, -1)$ check the options provided:

$g(x) = 2x + 1 \rightarrow -1 = 2(1) + 1 \rightarrow -1 = 3 \qquad$ This is NOT true.

$g(x) = 2x - 1 \rightarrow -1 = 2(1) - 1 = 1 \qquad$ This is NOT true.

$g(x) = -2x + 1 \rightarrow -1 = 2(-1) + 1 \rightarrow -1 = -1$ This is true.

$g(x) = x + 2 \rightarrow -1 = 1 + 2 \rightarrow -1 = 3$    This is NOT true.

$g(x) = 2x + 2 \rightarrow -1 = 2(1) + 2 = 1$    This is NOT true.

## 7) Choice C is correct

Use distance formula: $Distance = Rate \times time \Rightarrow 420 = 50 \times T$, divide both sides by 50. $420 \div 50 = T \Rightarrow T = 8.4\ hours$.Change hours to minutes for the decimal part. $0.4\ hours = 0.4 \times 60 = 24\ minutes$.

## 8) Choice B is correct.

Simplify the expression. $\sqrt{\frac{x^2}{2} + \frac{x^2}{16}} = \sqrt{\frac{8x^2}{16} + \frac{x^2}{16}} = \sqrt{\frac{9x^2}{16}} = \sqrt{\frac{9}{16}x^2} = \sqrt{\frac{9}{16}} \times \sqrt{x^2} = \frac{3}{4} \times x = \frac{3x}{4}$

## 9) Choice D is correct

To find the $y-$intercept of a line from its equation, put the equation in slope-intercept form:

$x - 3y = 12,\ -3y = -x + 12,\ \ \ \ \ 3y = x - 12,\ \ \ \ \ \ \ \ \ y = \frac{1}{3}x - 4$

The $y-$intercept is what comes after the $x$. Thus, the $y-$intercept of the line is $-4$.

## 10) Choice C is correct

Adding both side of $4a - 3 = 17$ by 3 gives $4a = 20$

Divide both side of $4a = 20$ by 4 gives $a = 5$, then $6a = 6(5) = 30$

## 11) Choice E is correct

The perimeter of the trapezoid is 54.

Therefore, the missing side (height) is $= 54 - 18 - 12 - 14 = 10$

Area of the trapezoid: $A = \frac{1}{2} h (b_1 + b_2) = \frac{1}{2} (10) (12 + 14) = 130$

## 12) Choice C is correct

Let $x$ be the number. Write the equation and solve for $x$. $\frac{2}{3} \times 18 = \frac{2}{5} . x \Rightarrow \frac{2 \times 18}{3} = \frac{2x}{5}$, use cross multiplication to solve for $x$. $5 \times 36 = 2x \times 3 \Rightarrow 180 = 6x \Rightarrow x = 30$

## 13) Choice B is correct

The easiest way to solve this one is to plug the answers into the equation.

When you do this, you will see the only time $x = x^{-6}$ is when $x = 1$ or $x = 0$.

Only $x = 1$ is provided in the choices.

**14) Choice C is correct**

First find a common denominator for both of the fractions in the expression $\frac{5}{x^2} + \frac{7x-3}{x^3}$.

of $x^3$, we can combine like terms into a single numerator over the denominator:

$$\frac{5x+4}{x^3} + \frac{7x-3}{x^3} = \frac{(5x+4)+(7x-3)}{x^3} = \frac{12x+1}{x^3}$$

**15) Choice D is correct**

Let's find the vertex of each choice provided:
A.  $y = 3x^2 - 3$    The vertex is: $(0, -3)$
B.  $y = -3x^2 + 3$    The vertex is: $(0, 3)$
C.  $y = x^2 + 3x - 3$
The value of $x$ of the vertex in the equation of a quadratic in standard form is: $x = \frac{-b}{2a} = \frac{-3}{2}$
(The standard equation of a quadratic is: $ax^2 + bx + c = 0$)
The value of $x$ in the vertex is 3 not $\frac{-3}{2}$.
D.  $y = 4(x - 3)^2 - 3$
Vertex form of a parabola equation is in form of $y = a(x - h)^2 + k$, where $(h, k)$ is the vertex.
Then $h = 3$ and $k = -3$. (This is the answer)
$E. y = 4x^2 + 3x - 3. x = \frac{-b}{2a} = \frac{-3}{2 \times 8} = -\frac{3}{16}$. The value of $x$ in the vertex is 3 not $-\frac{3}{16}$.

**16) Choice B is correct**

Use the information provided in the question to draw the shape.

Use Pythagorean Theorem: $a^2 + b^2 = c^2$

$40^2 + 30^2 = c^2 \Rightarrow 1600 + 900 = c^2 \Rightarrow 2500 = c^2 \Rightarrow c = 50$

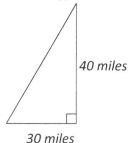

40 miles

30 miles

**17) Choice D is correct**

To find the average of three numbers even if they're algebraic expressions, add them up and divide by 3. Thus, the average equals: $\frac{(4x+2)+(-6x-5)+(8x+2)}{3} = \frac{6x-1}{3} = 2x - \frac{1}{3}$

**18) Choice B is correct**

If the score of Mia was 60, therefore the score of Ava is 30. Since, the score of Emma was half as that of Ava, therefore, the score of Emma is 15.

**19) Choice B is correct**

Let $x$ be the smallest number. Then, these are the numbers: $x, x+1, x+2, x+3, x+4$

$average = \frac{\text{sum of terms}}{\text{number of terms}} \Rightarrow 38 = \frac{x+(x+1)+(x+2)+(x+3)+(x+4)}{5} \Rightarrow 38 = \frac{5x+10}{5} \Rightarrow 190 = 5x + 10 \Rightarrow 180 = 5x \Rightarrow x = 36$

**20) Choice B is correct.**

Let $x$ be the number of adult tickets and $y$ be the number of student tickets. Then:

$x + y = 12,$         $12.50x + 7.50y = 125$

Use elimination method to solve this system of equation. Multiply the first equation by $-7.5$ and add it to the second equation. $-7.5(x + y = 12),$     $-7.5x - 7.5y = -90,$
$12.50x + 7.50y = 125.$   $5x = 35,$     $x = 7$

There are 7 adult tickets and 5 student tickets.

**21) Choice C is correct**

Write the ratio of $5a$ to $2b$. $\frac{5a}{2b} = \frac{1}{10}$

Use cross multiplication and then simplify. $5a \times 10 = 2b \times 1 \rightarrow 50a = 2b \rightarrow a = \frac{2b}{50} = \frac{b}{25}$

Now, find the ratio of $a$ to $b$. $\frac{a}{b} = \frac{\frac{b}{25}}{b} \rightarrow \frac{b}{25} \div b = \frac{b}{25} \times \frac{1}{b} = \frac{b}{25} = \frac{1}{25}$

**22) Choice C is correct**

4% of the volume of the solution is alcohol. Let $x$ be the volume of the solution.

Then: $4\% \ of \ x = 24 \ ml \Rightarrow 0.04 \ x = 24 \Rightarrow x = 24 \div 0.04 = 600$

**23) Choice B is correct**

$average = \frac{sum \ of \ terms}{number \ of \ terms}$, The sum of the weight of all girls is: $18 \times 60 = 1080 \ kg$, The sum of the weight of all boys is: $32 \times 62 = 1984 \ kg$, The sum of the weight of all students is: $1080 + 1984 = 3064 \ kg$, average $= \frac{3064}{50} = 61.28$

**24) Choice A is correct**

Plug in the value of $x$ in the equation and solve for $y$.

$$2y = \frac{2x^2}{3} + 6 \rightarrow 2y = \frac{2(9)^2}{3} + 6 \rightarrow 2y = \frac{2(81)}{3} + 6 \rightarrow 2y = 54 + 6 = 60$$
$$2y = 60 \rightarrow y = 30$$

**25) Choice A is correct**

Since a box of pen costs \$3, then $3p$ Represents the cost of $p$ boxes of pen.

Multiplying this number times 1.085 will increase the cost by the 8.5% for tax.

Then add the \$6 shipping fee for the total: $1.085(3p) + 6$

**26) Choice E is correct**

$$average = \frac{\text{sum of terms}}{\text{number of terms}} \Rightarrow 18 = \frac{13+15+20+x}{4} \Rightarrow 72 = 48 + x \Rightarrow x = 24$$

### 27) Choice C is correct

Let $x$ be the original price. If the price of the sofa is decreased by 25% to $420, then: $75\% \ of \ x = 420 \Rightarrow 0.75x = 420 \Rightarrow x = 420 \div 0.75 = 560$

### 28) Choice C is correct

Use simple interest formula: $I = prt$, ($I =$ interest, $p =$ principal, $r =$ rate, $t =$ time)

$$I = (8,000)(0.045)(5) = 1,800$$

### 29) Choice E is correct

$$(4.2 \times 10^6) \times (2.6 \times 10^{-5}) = (4.2 \times 2.6) \times (10^6 \times 10^{-5}) = 10.92 \times (10^{6 + (-5)})$$
$$= 1.092 \times 10^2$$

### 30) Choice D is correct

Rate of change (growth or $x$) is 15 per week. $45 \div 3 = 15$

Since the plant grows at a linear rate, then the relationship between the height ($y$) of the plant and number of weeks of growth ($x$) can be written as: $y(x) = 15x$

### 31) Choice E is correct

Simplify: $4(x + 1) = 6(x - 4) + 20, 4x + 4 = 6x - 24 + 20, 4x + 4 = 6x - 4$

Subtract $4x$ from both sides: $4 = 2x - 4$, Add 4 to both sides: $8 = 2x, 4 = x$

### 32) Choice E is correct

Use distributive property: $2x(4 + 2y) = 8x + 4xy = 4xy + 8x$

### 33) Choice E is correct

$y = 4ab + 3b^3$, plug in the values of $a$ and $b$ in the equation: $a = 2$ and $b = 3$,

$$y = 4(2)(3) + 3(3)^3 = 24 + 3(27) = 24 + 81 = 105$$

### 34) Choice E is correct

Based on corresponding members from two matrices, we get: $\begin{cases} 2x = x + 3y - 5 \\ 4x = 2y - 10 \end{cases} \rightarrow$

$\begin{cases} x - 3y = -5 \\ 4x - 2y = 10 \end{cases}$

Multiply first equation by $-4$. $\begin{cases} -4x + 12y = 20 \\ 4x - 2y = 10 \end{cases} \rightarrow$ add two equations.

$$10y = 30 \rightarrow y = 3 \rightarrow x = 4 \rightarrow x \times y = 12$$

**35) Choice C is correct.**

To solve for $f\left(3g(P)\right)$, first, find $3g(p)$: $g(x) = log_3 x \rightarrow g(p) = log_3 p \rightarrow 3g(p) =$

$3log_3 p = log_3 p^3$. Now, find $f(3g(p))$: $f(x) = 3^x \rightarrow f(log_3 p^3) = 3^{log_3 p^3}$

Logarithms and exponentials with the same base cancel each other. This is true because logarithms and exponentials are inverse operations. Then: $f(log_3 p^3) = 3^{log_3 p^3} = p^3$

**36) Choice D is correct**

A. $f(x) = x^2 - 5$     if     $x = 1 \rightarrow f(1) = (1)^2 - 5 = 1 - 5 = -4 \neq 5$

B. $f(x) = x^2 - 1$     if     $x = 1 \rightarrow f(1) = (1)^2 - 1 = 1 - 1 = 0 \neq 5$

C. $f(x) = \sqrt{x + 2}$     if     $x = 1 \rightarrow f(1) = \sqrt{1 + 2} = \sqrt{3} \neq 5$

D. $f(x) = \sqrt{x} + 4$     if     $x = 1 \rightarrow f(1) = \sqrt{1} + 4 = 5$

E. $f(x) = \sqrt{x} + 6$     if     $x = 1 \rightarrow f(1) = \sqrt{1} + 6 \neq 5$

**37) Choice B is correct**

Plug in each pair of number in the equation:

A. $(2, 1)$:                  $2\,(2) + 4\,(1) = 8$
B. $(-1, 3)$:            $2\,(-1) + 4\,(3) = 10$
C. $(-2, 2)$:            $2\,(-2) + 4\,(2) = 4$
D. $(2, 2)$:                  $2\,(2) + 4\,(2) = 12$
E. $(2, 8)$:                  $2\,(2) + 4\,(8) = 36$

Only Choice B is correct.

**38) Choice B is correct.**

A linear equation is a relationship between two variables, $x$ and $y$, and can be written in the form of $y = mx + b$. A non-proportional linear relationship takes on the form $y = mx + b$, where $b \neq 0$ and its graph is a line that does not cross through the origin. Only in graph B, the line does not pass through the origin

**39) Choice D is correct**

The relationship among all sides of special right triangle

$30° - 60° - 90°$ is provided in this triangle:

In this triangle, the opposite side of $30°$ angle is half of the hypotenuse.

Draw the shape of this question:

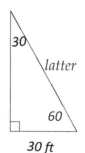

The latter is the hypotenuse. Therefore, the latter is $60\ ft$

### 40) Choice B is correct.

By definition, the sine of any acute angle is equal to the cosine of its complement.

Since, angle A and B are complementary angles, therefore: $\sin A\ =\ \cos B$

### 41) Choice C is correct

**Method 1:** Plugin the values of $x$ and $y$ provided in the options into both equations.

A. $(4,3)$                $x + y = 0 \rightarrow 4 + 3 \neq 0$
B. $(5,4)$                $x + y = 0 \rightarrow 5 + 4 \neq 0$
C. $(4,-4)$             $x + y = 0 \rightarrow 4 + (-4) = 0$
D. $(4,-6)$             $x + y = 0 \rightarrow 4 + (-6) \neq 0$
E. $(2,-6)$             $x + y = 0 \rightarrow 2 + (-6) \neq 0$

Only option C is correct.

**Method 2:** Multiplying each side of $x + y = 0$ by 2 gives $2x + 2y = 0$. Then, adding the corresponding side of $2x + 2y = 0$ and $4x - 2y = 24$ gives $6x = 24$. Dividing each side of $6x = 24$ by 6 gives $x = 4$. Finally, substituting 4 for $x$ in $x + y = 0$, or $y = -4$. Therefore, the solution to the given system of equations is $(4, -4)$.

### 42) Choice A is correct

If $f(x) = 3x + 4(x + 1) + 2$, then find $f(3x)$ by substituting $3x$ for every $x$ in the function. This gives: $f(3x) = 3\ (3x) + 4(3x + 1) + 2$

It simplifies to: $f(3x) = 3\ (3x) + 4(3x + 1) + 2 = 9x + 12x + 4 + 2 = 21x + 6$

### 43) Choice C is correct

First, find the equation of the line. All lines through the origin are of the form $y = mx$, so the equation is $y = \frac{2}{3}x$. Of the given choices, only choice C (9,6), satisfies this equation:

$$y = \frac{2}{3}x \rightarrow 6 = \frac{2}{3}(9) = 6$$

### 44) Choice C is correct

$(3n^2 + 4n + 6) - (2n^2 - 5).$         Add like terms together: $3n^2 - 2n^2 = n^2$

$4n$ doesn't have like terms. $6 - (-5) = 11$

Combine these terms into one expression to find the answer: $n^2 + 4n + 11$

### 45) Choice C is correct

You can find the possible values of $a$ and $b$ in $(ax + 4)(bx + 3)$ by using the given equation $a + b = 7$ and finding another equation that relates the variables $a$ and $b$. Since $(ax + 4)(bx + 3) = 10x^2 + cx + 12$, expand the left side of the equation to obtain

$abx^2 + 4bx + 3ax + 12 = 10x^2 + cx + 12$

Since $ab$ is the coefficient of $x^2$ on the left side of the equation and 10 is the coefficient of $x^2$ on the right side of the equation, it must be true that $ab = 10$

The coefficient of $x$ on the left side is $4b + 3a$ and the coefficient of $x$ in the right side is c. Then: $4b + 3a = c$,   $a + b = 7$, then: $a = 7 - b$

Now, plug in the value of a in the equation $ab = 10$. Then:

$ab = 10 \rightarrow (7 - b)b = 10 \rightarrow 7b - b^2 = 10$

Add $-7b + b^2$ both sides. Then: $b^2 - 7b + 10 = 0$

Solve for b using the factoring method. $b^2 - 7b + 10 = 0 \rightarrow (b - 5)(b - 2) = 0$

Thus, either $b = 2$ and $a = 5$, or $b = 5$ and $a = 2$. If $b = 2$ and $a = 5$, then

$4b + 3a = c \rightarrow 4(2) + 3(5) = c \rightarrow c = 23$. If $5 = 2$ and $a = 2$, then, $4b + 3a = c \rightarrow 4(5) + 3(2) = c \rightarrow c = 26$.   Therefore, the two possible values for $c$ are 23 and 26.

### 46) Choice A is correct

To rewrite $\frac{1}{\frac{1}{x-6}+\frac{1}{x+4}}$, first simplify $\frac{1}{x-6} + \frac{1}{x+4}$.

$\frac{1}{x-6} + \frac{1}{x+4} = \frac{1(x+4)}{(x-6)(x+4)} + \frac{1(x-5)}{(x+4)(x-6)} = \frac{(x+4)+(x-6)}{(x+4)(x-6)}$

Then: $\frac{1}{\frac{1}{x-6}+\frac{1}{x+4}} = \frac{1}{\frac{(x+4)+(x-6)}{(x+4)(x-6)}} = \frac{(x-6)(x+4)}{(x-6)+(x+4)}$. (Remember, $\frac{1}{\frac{1}{x}} = x$)

This result is equivalent to the expression in choice A.

### 47) Choice B is correct

Since $(0, 0)$ is a solution to the system of inequalities, substituting 0 for $x$ and 0 for $y$ in the given system must result in two true inequalities. After this substitution, $y < a - x$ becomes $0 < a$, and $y > x + b$ becomes $0 > b$. Hence, $a$ is positive and $b$ is negative. Therefore, $a > b$.

### 48) Choice D is correct

First find the slope of the line using the slope formula. $m = \frac{y_2 - y_1}{x_2 - x_1}$

Substituting in the known information. $(x_1, y_1) = (2, 4)$,   $(x_2, y_2) = (4,5)$

$m = \frac{5-4}{4-2} = \frac{1}{2}$

Now the slope to find the equation of the line passing through these points. $y = mx + b$

Choose one of the points and plug in the values of $x$ and $y$ in the equation to solve for $b$.

Let's choose point $(4, 5)$. Then: $y = mx + b \rightarrow 5 = \frac{1}{2}(4) + b \rightarrow 5 = 2 + b \rightarrow b = 5 - 2 = 3$

The equation of the line is: $y = \frac{1}{2}x + 3$

Now, plug in the points provided in the choices into the equation of the line.

A. $(9,9)$ $\quad y = \frac{1}{2}x + 3 \to 9 = \frac{1}{2}(9) + 3 \to 9 = 7.5$ $\quad$ This is NOT true.

B. $(9,6)$ $\quad y = \frac{1}{2}x + 3 \to 6 = \frac{1}{2}(9) + 3 \to 6 = 7.5$ $\quad$ This is NOT true.

C. $(6,9)$ $\quad y = \frac{1}{2}x + 3 \to 9 = \frac{1}{2}(6) + 3 \to 9 = 6$ $\quad$ This is NOT true.

D. $(6,6)$ $\quad y = \frac{1}{2}x + 3 \to 6 = \frac{1}{2}(6) + 3 \to 6 = 6$ $\quad$ This is true!

E. $(0,9)$ $\quad y = \frac{1}{2}x + 3 \to 9 = \frac{1}{2}(0) + 3 \to 9 = 3$ $\quad$ This is NOT true.

Therefore, the only point from the choices that lies on the line is $(6,6)$.

### 49) Choice B is correct

The input value is 4. Then: $x = 4$

$f(x) = x^2 - 3x \to f(4) = 4^2 - 3(4) = 16 - 12 = 4$

### 50) Choice B is correct

To solve this problem, first recall the equation of a line: $y = mx + b$

Where $m = slope.$ $\quad y = y - intercept$

Remember that slope is the rate of change that occurs in a function and that the $y-$intercept is the $y$ value corresponding to $x = 0$. Since the height of John's plant is 6 inches tall when he gets it. Time (or $x$) is zero. The plant grows 4 inches per year. Therefore, the rate of change of the plant's height is 4. The $y-$intercept represents the starting height of the plant which is 6 inches.

### 51) Choice C is correct

Multiplying each side of $\frac{3}{x} = \frac{12}{x-9}$ by $x(x-9)$ gives $3(x-9) = 12(x)$, distributing the 3 over the values within the parentheses yields $x - 9 = 4x$ or $x = -3$.

Therefore, the value of $\frac{x}{6} = \frac{-3}{6} = -\frac{1}{2}$.

### 52) Choice D is correct

The equation of a circle can be written as $(x-h)^2 + (y-k)^2 = r^2$
where $(h,k)$ are the coordinates of the center of the circle and $r$ is the radius of the circle. Since the coordinates of the center of the circle are $(0,4)$, the equation is $x^2 + (y-4)^2 = r^2$, where $r$ is the radius. The radius of the circle is the distance from the center $(0,4)$, to the given endpoint of a radius, $\left(\frac{5}{3},6\right)$. By the distance formula, $r^2 = \left(\frac{5}{3} - 0\right)^2 + (6-4)^2 = \frac{61}{9}$

Therefore, an equation of the given circle is $x^2 + (y-4)^2 = \frac{61}{9}$

### 53) Choice C is correct

To solve for $\cos A$ first identify what is known. The question states that $\triangle ABC$ is a right triangle whose $n \angle B = 90°$ and $\sin C = \frac{2}{3}$. It is important to recall that any triangle has a sum of interior angles that equals 180 degrees. Therefore, to calculate $\cos A$ use the complimentary angles identify of trigonometric function. $\cos A = \cos(90 - C)$, Then: $\cos A = \sin C$

For complementary angles, $sin$ of one angle is equal to $cos$ of the other angle. $\cos A = \frac{2}{3}$

## 54) Choice C is correct

In order to figure out what the equation of the graph is, fist find the vertex. From the graph we can determine that the vertex is at $(1,2)$. We can use vertex form to solve for the equation of this graph. Recall vertex form, $y = a(x - h)^2 + k$, where $h$ is the $x$ coordinate of the vertex, and $k$ is the $y$ coordinate of the vertex. Plugging in our values, you get $= a(x - 1)^2 + 2$, To solve for $a$, we need to pick a point on the graph and plug it into the equation. Let's pick $(-1, 10)$, $10 = a(-1 - 1)^2 + 2$

$10 = a(-2)^2 + 2$, $\qquad\qquad 10 = 4a + 2$, $\qquad 8 = 4a$, $\qquad a = 2$

Now the equation is : $y = 2(x - 1)^2 + 2$

Let's expand this, $y = 2(x^2 - 2x + 1) + 2$, $y = 2x^2 - 4x + 2 + 2$

$y = 2x^2 - 4x + 4$. $\qquad\qquad$ The equation in Choice C is the same.

## 55) Choice C is correct

The line passes through the origin, $(6, m)$ and $(m, 12)$. Any two of these points can be used to find the slope of the line. Since the line passes through $(0,0)$ and $(6, m)$, the slope of the line is equal to $\frac{m-0}{6-0} = \frac{m}{6}$. Similarly, since the line passes through $(0,0)$ and $(m, 12)$, the slope of the line is equal to $\frac{12-0}{m-0} = \frac{12}{m}$. Since each expression gives the slope of the same line, it must be true that $\frac{m}{6} = \frac{12}{m}$, Using cross multiplication gives

$\frac{m}{6} = \frac{12}{m} \rightarrow m^2 = 72 \rightarrow m = \pm\sqrt{72} = \pm\sqrt{36 \times 2} = \pm\sqrt{36} \times \sqrt{2} = \pm 6\sqrt{2}$

## 56) Choice B is correct

It is given that $g(6) = 4$. Therefore, to find the value of $f(g(6))$, then $f(g(6)) = f(4) = 7$

## 57) Choice A is correct

Area of the triangle is: $\frac{1}{2}\ AD \times BC$ and AD is perpendicular to $BC$. Triangle $ADC$ is a $30° - 60° - 90°$ right triangle. The relationship among all sides of right triangle $30° - 60° - 90°$ is provided in the following triangle: In this triangle, the opposite side of $30°$ angle is half of the hypotenuse. And the opposite side of $60°$ is opposite of $30° \times \sqrt{3}$

$CD = 4$, then $AD = 4 \times \sqrt{3}$

Area of the triangle $ABC$ is: $\frac{1}{2}\ AD \times BC = \frac{1}{2}\ 4\sqrt{3} \times 8 = 16\sqrt{3}$

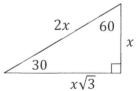

## 58) Choice C is correct

It is given that $g(7) = 8$. Therefore, to find the value of $f(g(7))$, substitute 8 for $g(7)$. $f(g(7)) = f(8) = 35$.

**59) Choice C is correct**

The equation of a circle in standard form is: $(x - h)^2 + (y - k)^2 = r^2$, where $r$ is the radius of the circle. In this circle the radius is 4. $r^2 = 16 \rightarrow r = 4$, $(x + 2)^2 + (y - 4)^2 = 16$

Area of a circle: $A = \pi r^2 = \pi (4)^2 = 16\pi$

**60) Choice B is correct**

By definition, the sine of any acute angle is: $sin\ A = \frac{opposite}{adjacent} = \frac{a}{c}$. Only choice B is correct.

## "Effortless Math Education" Publications

Effortless Math authors' team strives to prepare and publish the best quality CLEP College Algebra learning resources to make learning Math easier for all. We hope that our publications help you learn Math in an effective way and prepare for the CLEP College Algebra test.

We all in Effortless Math wish you good luck and successful studies!

Effortless Math Authors

# www.EffortlessMath.com

... So Much More Online!

- ✓ FREE Math lessons

- ✓ More Math learning books!

- ✓ Mathematics Worksheets

- ✓ Online Math Tutors

**Need a PDF version of this book?**

Visit www.EffortlessMath.com

Made in the USA
Coppell, TX
22 February 2020